MANAGE YOUR MIND

MANAGE YOUR MIND

For Emotional Intelligence, Feelings,
Moods, and Stress Management

Anurag P. Lakhlani

PARTRIDGE
A Penguin Random House Company

To order additional copies of this book, contact
Partridge India
000 800 10062 62
orders.india@partridgepublishing.com

www.partridgepublishing.com/india

CONTENTS

Part I: Why We Need Mind Management

Part II: Quick Action Tools

Part III: Deep Action Tools

Part IV: Mastering Emotional Intelligence

Part V: Managing Feelings and Moods

Part VI: Managing Stress

Part VII: Putting Things Together

List of Methods of Meditation in Chapter 14

List of Undesired Feelings and Moods Discussed in Chapter 23

List of Desired Feelings and Moods Discussed in Chapter 24

ACKNOWLEDGMENT

I take this opportunity to express my gratefulness to my parents. They have always supported and motivated me. I also express my gratitude for my sister Avni, her husband Nirav, and regards to their baby girl Utsavi.

There are many individuals who have influenced and shaped my life. I express my thanks to all of them. I especially remember Naran Muchhar, Mehul Bhatt, and Nagender Singh for their friendship.

Anurag Lakhlani

PART I

WHY WE NEED MIND MANAGEMENT

CHAPTER 1

Why Should You Read This Book?

"Why did my plant die?" a child asked his mother in disbelief. For the five-year-old, this plant in a small pot meant the world. "I have cleaned all the leaves daily, sprinkled water on them, put the plant in sunlight, given it food. Then why did it die?" Tears were rolling down his eyes.

With love, his mother embraced him and said, "Son, you needed to water the roots, not the leaves."

Emotions, feelings, and moods arise in the mind. Attempts to address them only at the behavioral, philosophical, or intellectual levels will not lead us to deeper success. When the crisis strikes, all superficial learning will evaporate and the core of the character will be exposed to the situation. We need to water the roots. We need to learn to manage our mind—conscious and subconscious. We need to find out what influences the state of mind, the thoughts, the moods, the feelings, and the emotions. We need to build the paradigm, the belief system, the character, self-identity, the understanding of self, and purpose of life to become emotionally intelligent in a deeper sense. If we understand how to manage the mind, we will be better equipped to manage emotions, feelings, moods, and deal with stress.

This book is a practical and common-sense approach to understand and manage the mind for the above purposes.

I like the following story:

"I can speak ten languages fluently. Can anyone figure out which one is my mother tongue?" a foreign scholar challenged the court of a king.

The king, who always promoted scholarly interactions and challenges, asked his court to figure out the mother tongue of the foreign scholar. All the wise men in the court tried to test his knowledge of the language, his fluency, his vocabulary, his grammar, his accent. The foreign scholar demonstrated his proficiency in all ten languages that a native speaker has. All day long, the wise men tried and failed to figure out the mother tongue.

When all failed, the prime minister stood up and said, "Please be our guest for a night. If we fail to identify your mother tongue by tomorrow noon, you win."

The king was also enjoying the battle and was hopeful that his prime minister would solve this puzzle.

In the middle of the night, when the foreign scholar was in deep sleep, the prime minister poured cold water on the scholar and started beating him abruptly. Confused by the situation, out of surprise and panic, the scholar asked in one language, "Why are you beating me?"

"The language you are speaking now is your mother tongue," claimed the prime minister.

The scholar agreed, praised the wisdom of the prime minister, and left the court in the morning.

In crisis, when we are not prepared, the inner reality comes out.

Can we develop a deeper character and proper understanding of mind such that we can face even crises more efficiently? This is what this book aims for.

What is in this book? What will you learn?

- Part 1: Why We Need Mind Management: This part introduces you to the need of the deeper understanding of the mind. It also introduces the tools we will develop in the following parts.

- Part 2: Quick Action Tools: Here, you will explore what can quickly influence the state of mind. You may want to upgrade your tools, which will be helpful for decreasing the intensity of an unwanted state of mind or increasing the intensity of a desired state of mind by quickly managing the state of mind.

- Part 3: Deep Action Tools: This part of the book will "water the roots" and develop a much deeper understanding of the mind. You will develop a much deeper understanding of self, life, conditioning of the mind, and learn the methods of meditation.

- Part 4: Mastering Emotional Intelligence: Here, we explore what emotional intelligence is. We develop a strategy—a master plan to manage emotions with the help of tools developed in parts 2 and 3. We explore selected groups of emotions one at a time for detailed analysis and discussion.

- Part 5: Managing Feelings and Moods: We explore selected feelings and moods. We understand them. Then, we may apply our tools to manage them efficiently.

- Part 6: Managing Stress: Here, we explore the world of stress. This book discusses some factors that may help reduce stress and manage it efficiently. The tools of parts 2 and 3 can be utilized to manage stress.

- Part 7: Living a Happy Life: This section concludes the learning of the book with anecdotes.

Benjamin Franklin wisely said, "Tell me and I forget, teach me and I may remember, involve me and I learn." For effective learning from this book, make sure you set some personal goals, read and contemplate on the material regularly, explore and participate in the activities of developing your tools actively.

Are you ready to take a deep dive into the world of "managing the mind?" Keep on reading.

CHAPTER 2

The Mysterious Mind

"What we achieve inwardly will change outer reality".

—Plutarch

How about exploring the following activities?

Activity 1: Close your eyes and observe how you feel. Are you relaxed, calm, or agitated? How are your body muscles? Do you feel any tension in hand, leg, or body muscles? How is your breathing? Is it deep or shallow? Observe all these and remember them.

Activity 2: Now, remember the worst incident of your life for a minute. It can be a job loss, a betrayal in love, social insult, or any other situation. For just one minute, remember the details—rewind the movie: what you saw, heard, and felt at that time. What was your internal state of mind? Just remember.

Activity 3: Now, come out of the situation and take inventory of the body and mind again. Compare with the situation after Activity 1. Are you relaxed and calm or agitated? How about your muscles and breathing? I bet, just by remembering an incident, your state of mind will change. The emotions, feelings, and mood will change. So, may we conclude that one of the factors that can affect our mind quickly is "memory recall?"

Activity 4: Now, let us use the same mechanism of memory recall to get into a pleasant state. Remember the best incident of your life. It may be a memorable vacation, a memorable event in a relationship, winning a competition, any family gathering, or any other thing. Again, for just one minute, remember the details—rewind the movie to what you saw, heard, and felt at that time. Just remember. I bet, just by remembering this incident, your state of mind will change.

Activity 5: If you are not yet relaxed, do this breathing exercise. Just relax your body and take deep breaths. In deep breathing, your abdomen should move, not the chest. Take deep and longer breaths for a few minutes and take inventory of your body. I believe, by now, you are much more relaxed.

You may ask, what is the point in doing these activities? Well, I just wanted to demonstrate that there are factors that influence the state of mind. I wanted to give you an experience. I believe I have succeeded, at least partially, to convince you that we can change the state of mind by various activities and hence can manage our emotions, feelings, moods, etc.

I would classify the factors affecting mind in two categories, depending on how they can affect the mind.

1. Quick Action Tools: They influence the mind very fast.
2. Deep Action Tools: They influence the mind for the long term.

Here are some more details of both the above categories.

1. Quick Action Tools: The following diagram summarizes the activities that can influence the state of mind very quickly. In subsequent chapters, we will explore each of them individually.

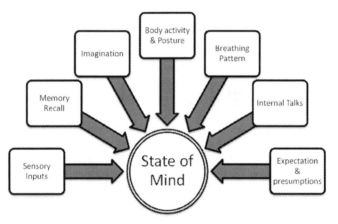

Figure: Quick Action Tools that can change the state of mind quickly

2. Deep Action Tools: The following diagram summarizes what influences the mind in the long term and has longer perspective. We will explore each of them individually in detail in this book.

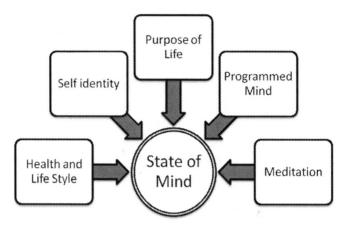

Figure: Deep Action Tools that can nurture
and develop the mind over a long time.

Lao Tzu said, "A journey of a thousand miles begins with a single step." Let us take one step at a time to understand our mind and manage it effectively.

> With help of the mind,
> I become happy, feel love,
> I remember; I imagine,
> Mind makes my life colorful.
>
> When the mind is uncontrolled,
> I feel fear, become jealous,
> I am worried and anxious,
> Mind gives me sorrow.
>
> Mind is a good helper,
> Mind is a painful ruler,
> Manage your mind,
> Or the mind will manage you.

PART II

QUICK ACTION TOOLS

CHAPTER 3

Sensory Inputs

Our senses are the doors to our mind.
Joy as well as jealousy can enter through it.

How do we interact with the world? Well, we use our five senses for the interaction. Anything we know about the world comes to us through one of the senses. These senses have great influence on the state of our mind. Let us explore all the senses and understand how we can utilize them to manage our mind.

1. Vision: When we see a car approaching us with full speed, an emotion of fear elicits in us and we jump away from the car. When we see a beautiful painting, we become delighted. When we don't see our car keys in its usual place, especially while getting late for work, we become irritated. When we read a romantic letter from our beloved one, love prevails over our mind. When we see an insulting e-mail, it makes us angry. Now, we are very sure that what we see impacts our state of mind and effectively influences the emotions, moods, and feelings. So, can we use this knowledge for our benefit?

When I am angry and upset, I spend some time with nature, especially during sunset. When I see the colorful sky, with the intricacies of the shades of the colors, I become delighted. What is your experience about such a colorful sky? When I see the photo album of my last vacation, a sense of happiness and delight comes to me. Do you keep pictures of your family and friends with you? What do you feel when you look at them?

When I am down and not energetic, I glance through the photos of award ceremonies where I received awards. This gives me courage. This gives me momentum and inspiration to work harder.

Here is the list of my tools that give me positive emotions, moods, and feelings if I look at them.

- Beautiful trees and flowers in a garden or park and other natural places.
- Pictures of children, family, and friends, especially during vacation trips.
- Pictures and news articles on my achievements.
- Photos of celebrities I admire, like Einstein, Steve Jobs, etc.
- Reading my favorite book.

Can you list the top five things that are visual in nature and can influence your emotions, moods, and feelings in a positive way?

Your tools:

1. _____
2. _____
3. _____
4. _____
5. _____

2. Hearing: When I hear a melodious song or music, I become happy. Once in a while, I go to natural places. When I hear the sounds of birds or the roaring of the ocean, I become refreshed and delighted. When someone praises me, I become proud. Do you remember any such situation in your life? Can you identify incidents when what you hear makes you happy?

At the same time, there is another side of the coin as well. If I hear words that are insulting to me, I become angry. When I hear the news that my endeavor has not become as successful as I wished, I become sad. Can you recall such incidents?

To achieve a positive state of mind, I have developed certain tools. Let me share what I do to elevate my mood and emotions if I am sad or angry.

My tools:

- I have a set of songs and music that make me happy.
- Natural sounds like the songs of birds, the flowing of a river, the roaring of the ocean
- Motivational talks by selected speakers

- Selected audio books
- Selected movies (audiovisual)

Your tools: Please list your top five sounds that can help manage your mood.

1. _____
2. _____
3. _____
4. _____
5. _____

3. Kinesthetic: When I feel water drops on my face, especially during the first rain of the season, I become delighted. When I am taking shower, I sometimes feel the water on my body and become relaxed. When I stroke a pet, I become relaxed playing with it. On the seashore, sometimes I just feel the waves by putting my hand in the water and the wet sand that has just seen the wave go. All these things make me happy. Do you have similar experiences?

On the other hand, if something hurts my palm, I become sad. Do you remember any new shoe that bit you? Any shirt that was too tight to feel comfortable?

Well, as you can now predict, I have tools for kinesthetic experiences that will bring out the desired state of my mind.

My tools:

- Feeling the water drops while taking a shower
- Stroking a pet

- Touching the smooth wet sand on a seashore
- Touching smooth grass
- Massage

Your tools: Top five kinesthetic means for positive state of mind.

1. _____
2. _____
3. _____
4. _____
5. _____

4. Smell: I don't like pungent smells. Whenever I come across such smells, it irritates me. When I pass near a garbage can, I don't like the smell. Such a smell makes me unpleasant. Do you remember any such experience?

On the positive side, the smell of my favorite perfume, the smell of the first rain of the season, the smell of the flower, and the smell of the food I love to eat make me happy.

Here are my tools that I have developed to create a positive impact on my mind using smell.

- Smell of fresh flowers
- My favorite perfume
- My favorite room freshener
- Smell of the food I love to eat
- Smell of water near a waterfall and the ocean

Your tools: Top five smell means for positive state of mind.

1. _____
2. _____
3. _____
4. _____
5. _____

5. *Gustatory*: For the purpose of the discussion for this book, I will extend the meaning of gustatory to taste as well as food we eat. If I taste something and it is very hot, I run for the water immediately. On the other hand, when someone presents me with chocolates, I become happy. What I eat and drink also influences my mind. It is not only limited to taste, but also depends on the contents of the food. Drinking excessive alcohol can affect the state of one's mind. There are many foods that can make me feel sleepy. Anesthesia can be created by smelling a chemical. The point I want to make is that along with taste, what I take in—gas, liquid, or solid, can influence the state of my mind. Let me create tools to induce a positive state of mind.

My tools:

- Taste of my favorite food
- Eating ice cream
- Eating chocolate
- Drinking fresh fruit juice
- Drinking my favorite coffee

Your tools: Top five gustatory things for positive state of mind.

1. _____
2. _____
3. _____
4. _____
5. _____

Make sure you also develop your tools along with mine.

6. *Multi-sensory Tools*: So far we have developed our tools for individual senses. Can we have a combined list of activities that we can do involving multiple senses? The following are my top five activities that help put me in a positive state of mind.

- Watching a movie or documentary film. I have list of my favorite movies.
- Watching video recordings of family functions, vacation trips.
- Surfing the Internet and social media. I have selected Web sites that I surf when I want to change my mood.
- Having my favorite lunch at my favorite restaurant.
- Calling a friend and talking with him.

What are your top five activities that involve one or more senses? Please prepare your tools.

Your tools:

1. _____
2. _____
3. _____
4. _____
5. _____

Our mind can be influenced by what we see, hear, touch, smell, and taste. If we select these inputs to the mind, the state of mind can be managed.

CHAPTER 4

Memory Recall

Memory recall is a double-edged sword.
It can help you. It can hurt you.

It was raining heavily while two monks were returning back to their monastery. They had to cross a small river which was flooding with fresh water. They saw a young woman waiting for the water to recede, as she was afraid to cross the river.

One of the monks helped the woman. He took her on his shoulders, crossed the river, and put her down on the other side. By that time, it was getting darker, and the monks reached their monastery.

After dinner, the second monk asked the first one, "We should not touch women. We are monks and our goal is to find the ultimate truth. We follow rules and our rules don't permit interaction with women. Why did you take the woman on your shoulders?"

"I left the woman on the other side of the river. Why are you still carrying her in your mind?" answered the first monk.

Memory recall is going back to our past. All of us have a past. This is stored in our mind as memories. Reflecting upon the past can trigger various emotions in us. The question is can we learn to recall the positive memory? If we can, it can help us to transform the state of the mind in positive way.

Now, let us explore how memory can create anger and stress. Then, we will explore how memory recall can trigger happiness and confidence. The focus of our discussion here is to realize that memory recall impacts the state of our mind.

Anger:

Scenario: It was the biggest insult Tom had ever faced. Tom's boss reprimanded him in front of the entire office staff for coming late to the office. Tom had his reasons for coming late, but his boss did not listen. He was upset the entire day. And the memory of this event was hurting him even after his dinner. He was very angry with his boss for such impolite behavior.

Comments: The anger in Tom can last for days or weeks. If he recalls this particular event of insult, he may become angry at any place and any time. The thing is the event has happened. Tom can't change it. The best approach for him would be to get over it as quickly as he can.

Do you recall any such memory that spoils your present moment? Let us examine such memories. Let us identify these memories so that we become aware of them. Once we are aware, once we know what causes anger, we are ready to take steps to prevent them.

Stress:

Scenario: Tom noticed that his boss's behavior was becoming aggravating day by day. For even small mistakes, he was insulted. Tom was no more enjoying his job. The periodic and repeated incidents were now building stress in him. He was unable to forget the memories of the office when he was home. The events replayed in his mind and made him more and more stressful. He became angry with his family without any reason and then realized that it was all because of his strained relation with his boss.

Comments: Stress due to unpleasant work life is very common. If our mind is occupied with office events even when we are home, it will take a toll. Stress will build up.

Many times, when something happens unexpectedly that we don't like, we spend nights remembering and reliving it. The sleepless nights induce stress. These unexpected things we don't like can be failure in a relationship, death of a loved one, or any incident where we can't achieve what we desire. Can you recall any such incident in your life? Does it make you stressful? Again, let us identify these events so that we can take preventive action.

Happiness:

Scenario: Tom decided to free himself from the memories of office life. He had a great collection of photographs of his birthday celebrations, New Year celebrations, his vacation trips, and more. He posted some of them on the wall, on the refrigerator, in the bedroom, so that he could recall the good memories of the past and become happy.

Comment: Almost all of us have memories that can make us happy. The question is if our mind goes to past memories anyway, why not remember something that will elicit positive emotions in us? I have a collection of photos, videos, selected things I collected on vacation trips, etc. When I look at them, they transport me to the past full of good memories and I become delighted. Do you have such a collection? If yes, what are you waiting for? Just utilize all those tools and become happy.

Confidence:

Scenario: Tom decided to change his job, as he was not comfortable in his job environment. He started applying for jobs. He started to get interview calls. At the time of the interviews, he recalled the memories of his successful student life. He was a very good student and used to face his verbal examinations very confidently. He correlated the verbal exams with interviews and became confident. So, he looked back into his student life, gained confidence, and faced the current interviews.

Comments: We all need confidence at one time or another. We all have become successful in doing something. It can be success in professional life, educational life, social life, personal life, or family life. We can recall the memories of the success. This will put us in a confident state.

When I want to gain confidence, I look back to my student and social life. I am sure you will also find such incidents and stories from your life.

Use of Triggers, Anchors, Cue for Memory Recall

If I analyze my thought patterns, I find that there are some cues, anchors, triggers that remind me of my past. Let us explore them so that we can learn how to trigger the right kind of memory recall.

- Sensory Inputs: If I look at photographs of my trips to mountain resorts, I become delighted. If I listen to the song that was played at my favorite party; I recall that event. If I listen to any word or phrase, that also reminds me of things. Similarly, smell, taste, and kinesthetic inputs make me dive into the past. Knowing this, I can use sensory inputs to guide my thoughts.

- Special Anchors: I may have special anchors to remind me of something good. These special anchors can simply be a sentence I write down and put on my desk so that I can see it frequently.

My memory recall tools: Let me share my top five memory recall tips that put me in a positive state of mind.

- My family gathering during celebrations.
- My participation in sports events during my school days.
- Memories of a visit to Lake Tahoe when I was in California.
- My leadership roles during school days.
- The most interesting final match I saw on television.

Your tools: List the top five memory recalls for a positive state of mind.

1. _____
2. _____
3. _____
4. _____
5. _____

CHAPTER 5

Imagination

One day, I imagined becoming a writer.
Then, this book came to existence.

If I define the "memory recall" as reliving an event in my mind that has already happened, I would define "imagination" as living or visualizing an event, achievement, etc. that has not happened.

We are dreamers. We imagine, fantasize, hallucinate, visualize, and project things that do not exist and events that have not happened. We imagined that we could fly and we built airplanes. We imagined that we could walk on the moon, and we went to the moon. All achievers have the power of visualization and imagination.

If we come back to everyday life, this power of imagination works in two ways to influence the state of our mind. Sometimes it creates positive states of mind; other times, it creates negative states of mind.

Anxiety:

Scenario: Ever since Maria knew her father had diabetes, she was worried about his health. Her father already had high blood pressure. Maria's father lived alone in his farmhouse. She always feared whether he was in any medical danger. Did he take his medicine regularly? Was he meeting the family doctor regularly? And what if there is an emergency? The hospital was far from the farmhouse. All these thoughts kept her worried, and the worries and fears developed into anxiety. She always imagined worst-case scenarios that made her worried.

Comment: Once in a while, we get anxious about something. If we think negatively, this will be the result. The key is to shift the imagination positively.

Happiness and excitement:

Scenario: Judy and Bill have planned their vacation. They will be going to their favorite mountain resort. Judy was busy dreaming about it. She imagined them walking through the wilderness, holding hands, stopping near a river, sitting on a stone on the river bank, and sharing their deepest desires and dreams. Those days, her eyes were full or dreams and the sheer thought of the vacation made her happy and excited.

Comment: Most of us dream about various things. The subject of our imaginations may vary, like marrying our dream partner, having a dream job, owning a beautiful house, going on vacations, success in career, etc. When we dream positively, it gives us hope and makes us happy. If you are not happy with your current job, you may imagine or dream about finding one that you like and a happy life after it. If you are not happy about any life situation, you may imagine the good situation and elevate your mood.

Do you have such dreams and imaginations that can make you happy? If not, it is time to list them out.

My tools: The following are my top five imaginative ideas with which I maintain my positive state of mind. Many of them might look silly, but they work for me.

- When I am anxious, I imagine that I have put all my worries in a box. I close the box, give it to God, and then I go to sleep. I become relaxed and sleep comfortably.

- When I fail to achieve my goal several times, I imagine Thomas Edison as my mentor. I ask myself, "What would Edison do if he failed in this endeavor a few times?"
  "Keep trying with different approaches and innovation." I get this answer in my mind. This gives me courage.

- When I am dejected, I watch an adventurous movie. I imagine all the great things that the protagonist achieves.

- If I am in a sad mood, I project a positive future full of success. I imagine what if I achieved all my dreams? How happy would I be? Thinking of success puts my mind in a positive state.

- Guided imagination: If I am tired, I use guided imagination to relax. I imagine myself sitting on the seashore looking at the sunset. I imagine all the sensory inputs I would be experiencing if I were really sitting there.

Your tools: Top five imaginative ideas you want to have for a positive state of mind.

1. _____
2. _____
3. _____
4. _____
5. _____

In your imagination, you can crate anything and become anything. Why imagine anything other than the best? Of course, keep in mind that this exercise is for managing the state of your mind. Do not get lost in daydreaming. Use imagination so that it helps you. It is also a double-edged sword.

CHAPTER 6

Body Activities and Postures

When I am stressed out, I take a long walk.
It helps dilute the stress.

Mind and body influence each other. If your body gets sick, the mind does not operate at its best. Similarly, if you are angry, it influences the body and the blood pressure increases.

Try this activity without hurting your eyes. Observe how it influences the frequency of thoughts in your mind. Sit comfortably and relax. Close your eyes briefly to relax them. Then, gaze at something at arm's distance. You can use a mirror as well. If your eyes get tired, feel free to close them and relax. Then gaze again. You may observe that the breathing may slow down and the frequency of thought decreases.

There are many activities that you may do to bring your mind to a positive state. We will explore a few such bodily activities and postures. A few of them may look silly. In my opinion, if they help us, they are worth exploring.

- Dancing and singing: Can you become angry when you are dancing and singing your favorite song? Well, I can't. If you are worried, tired, or anxious, if you spend some time singing or dancing, does this alleviate your worry? If yes, then you may just sing to unburden yourself. You may just take a few dancing steps in private (or in public at the right place and time) and can observe that your mood shifts positively.

- Sports: I like to play table tennis, tennis, badminton, etc. When I play, it is lot of work and my focus is on the game. Somehow, all the stress of my busy work life becomes less. Do you have your favorite sports that you play to relax?

- Aerobic exercises: I believe exercise is good for physical as well as mental health. I have my weekly schedule for exercise. After exercising, I feel relaxed. How about you?

- Walking, jogging, and swimming: When I have a busy day, I go for a long walk. Fast walking for about half an hour is my favorite activity after having an involving day. You may also choose to jog. In all these cases, the tension, worries, etc. are reduced.

- Yoga and yoga postures: Yoga has become popular these days due to various benefits. You may choose any specific type of yoga.

- Massage: This is another way to get relaxed.

- Playing music, painting, and any other artistic activity can also change the state of mind.

- Progressive relaxation: This is a mind-body activity. I do progressive relaxation frequently, and I get relaxed after this activity. How about you? Do you want to find a guided progressive relaxation? Or you may have your own customized one.

- Special activities like (a) laughing out loud in front of a mirror; (b) raising your hand and saying "yes" in front of a mirror; (c) making faces in front of a mirror; (d) taking extended showers, enjoying the water; (e) silently walking either during sunrise or sunset and observing nature; (f) lying down relaxed listening to soft music; (g) spending quality time with family, kids, friends.

If you observe, there may be many more activities in your life that are making you happy. List them. Utilize them to manage the mind.

Your tools: Mention your top five body activities and postures that can help your mind acquire a positive state.

1. _____

2. _____

3. _____
4. _____
5. _____

Our existence is psychosomatic. By changing one aspect—the body—the other aspect—the mind—can be influenced as well. We need to find out how to fine-tune the mind by changing the body positions, postures, and activities.

CHAPTER 7

Breathing Patterns

I find it difficult to become angry
when I am breathing deeply.

Whenever I am anxious, worried, or angry due to anything, I take deep breaths. I increase the time duration of inhalation and exhalation. The pace of the breathing is slow to medium. During breathing, the abdomen moves in and out and my chest remains almost still.

In the East, there are numerous meditation techniques based on breathing. Sages have realized the relation between the state of mind and the breathing pattern. What could cause this relation? There might be many reasons. I think our body is like a system. If one aspect of the body-mind changes, the other aspects also change. For example, if I am angry, my body rhythm changes. In anger, the blood pressure, breathing, facial expression, etc. changes and reflects the state of anger. So, mind has influence over body. Is the reverse true? Well, it may or may not be true for all processes. As far as breathing is concerned, it seems to be true. Changing the breathing rhythm changes the state of mind.

Breathing is a useful tool to manage the mind and hence influence emotions, feelings, and moods. The following are some selected breathing patterns.

- Relax and calm breathing: You might be anywhere in any situation. Simply be relaxed and slow down your breathing. Take deep breaths. Take normal inhalation and exhalation time durations. Stay in this position for a few minutes and you will observe that your mind calms down.

- Count the relaxed breaths: You may add variation in the above pattern. Just count the number of your breaths. This will keep your mind involved and reduce thoughts.

- Equal inhalation and exhalation times: You may time your inhalations and exhalations. Keep the breathing slow and deep. Make sure the time for inhalation and exhalation are the same. Make sure the breathing is comfortable and it does not create any additional stress in itself.

- Relax and calm your breathing before sleeping: Lie down on your bed and relax. Perform the relaxed and deep breathing technique for a few minutes before sleeping. This may improve the quality of sleep. Sound sleep is necessary for health as well as managing the mind.

CHAPTER 8

Internal Talks

"I think, therefore I am."

—Rene Descartes

"What could be the reasons for my low salary hike this year? I have done my best for the company." Tom was unable to digest the fact that his salary rise was just two percent. His mind was hyperactive and he was trying to figure out what went wrong. He decided to talk with his supervisor the next day.

"What should I say to him?" he was thinking. "I will give him the details of all the new clients I made this year. I will give him how much revenue my efforts have generated. This will convince George, and he will recommend a salary hike." Tom was happy to think of this positive outcome, but his happiness was short lived. "George may remind me of all the clients I have lost last year. He may point out the opportunity lost when I could not close the deal with that car company." His face was now tense. In his mind, he was thinking about all the possible dialogues with George. Delighted sometimes and sad other times, he was lost in the imaginary dialogues between him and his supervisor.

"I should have spent more time with Jill this weekend." Jake was continuously thinking about how he should have balanced work and personal life during the last weekend. "It was her birthday and I am the person she loves the most. She was planning for the weekend trip for a long time, but I could not go with her because of work." Jake was sad. He realized he missed the opportunity to spend some quality time with his wife.

The dialogues in his mind continued, "Well, in this tough economy, I need to take my job seriously. And if I make more money, it will eventually make Jill and me happy. Sometimes I need to sacrifice personal plans for better financial future." That was a reasonable thought and his face was normal. "Let me find out how I can make Jill happy. Well, she liked that red purse in that shop, but she did not buy it, as we did not have enough money. How about I buy her the purse as a gift?" Then, his face was delighted and he started planning how he would surprise Jill.

I have noticed a constant voice in my head. It is my permanent companion. I have also observed how these dialogues can influence my emotions, feelings, and moods.

Sometimes, they make me happy; other times, they make me sad. Do you have similar experiences?

What are some of the incidents that created dialogues in our minds? Let us list a few.

- Discussions with family, friends, colleagues, etc. that remained incomplete
- Discussions that did not end in satisfactory outcomes
- Heated discussions that went wrong and that we may wish to correct
- New proposals—personal or professional—that ended in unwanted outcomes
- Anticipations and preparations of crucial or delicate discussions that will happen in the future
- Incidents of insults, shame, guilt, defeats
- Incidents of happiness, fulfillment, achievement, victory, and pride
- Anxiety and nervousness while doing something new, or re-attempting something if we have failed previously
- Fear of failure and what others will say about my failure

What are some of the emotions that are elicited due to these dialogues? Well, here are a few.

- Happiness: vacations with the family that we rewind and replay in our minds; incidents of achievements.
- Anger: incidents where we feel cheated, treated unjustly, treated beneath our personal dignities.

- Confidence: reliving the memories of achievements.
- Sadness: incidents where we wished to say one thing but under pressure of time said another thing.
- Anxiety: anticipation of failure or that something may go wrong

How do we manage unwanted internal dialogues?

The mind is a chatterbox. I have observed that there is always something going on in my mind. The question is how can I make sure these dialogues keep me in a desired state of mind and not in unwanted and less resourceful states? The following are the steps that I take to make sure the dialogues in my mind are drawing positive energy into me.

1. Awareness of current dialogs in my mind by conscious observation
2. Acknowledgement and acceptance without fighting with the self
3. Aiming to change by deciding and asking, "Do I want to experience this state?"
4. Acting to change by accessing the positive memories and dialogues from my past

We can guide our internal talks. We can use any resource from sensory inputs, memory recall, or imaginative (including guided imagination with a positive outcome) tools. You can develop your own tools for guiding your internal talks.

CHAPTER 9

Expectations and Assumptions

"Expectations are the root of all heartache."
—William Shakespeare

Scenario: Mike likes pizzas. He has a favorite pizza restaurant. Whenever he goes to other restaurants, many of the times he returns unhappy and dissatisfied. Why? He always compares the taste of that pizza with his favorite pizza. And when he finds the difference, it makes him dissatisfied.

Comments: Now, you may realize that it is the expectation which is making him dissatisfied. He may approach this in different way. He may have his favorite pizza. At the same time, he may understand that all pizza restaurants are different. And the tastes will be different. He may enjoy the diversity of tastes, keeping his favorite taste untouched.

Scenario: Mike knows his boss is very demanding. If he makes a small mistake, his boss will insult him. The last evening, Mike made some mistakes in his assignment. The next day, his boss called him to discuss this issue. Mike was tense. He was expecting some heated discussions. He was mentally preparing to face another insult. But his boss was in a pleasant mood for some personal reason. He did not insult Mike. He guided Mike on how to avoid such mistakes. The discussion was to the point, objective, and professional. After the discussion, Mike was happy.

Comment: Why might Mike be happy? He had assumptions that his boss would insult him, but the situation turned out to be better than his assumption. So, even though the discussion was normal and professional, Mike was happy.

If our emotions and moods depend on our presuppositions, why not adjust them so that we are always happy? The event will unfold the way it would and we may have only partial control over the event, but if we can change our expectations and assumptions, we can be happier.

How many times have you observed that your expectations, assumptions, and presumptions have made you unhappy or put you in an undesired state of mind? Here is a list of a few possible expectations.

- I was expecting nice weather. We prepared for a picnic, but it rained and we could not go on a picnic. I was very frustrated. (Comment: I have no control over the weather. Why get frustrated?)

- I assumed Jack would come on time and we would go for dinner. But as usual, he came late. It disturbed all my plans after dinner. (Comment: If I know Jack's nature, why not prepare for delays?)
- I was in a hurry and took a certain highway. But there was a big traffic jam and I could not reach my destination on time. Why do such traffic jams happen? (Comment: Why assume less traffic on that highway?)

Here are a few more brief observations about negative emotions generated due to assumptions.

- Expectations from parents, siblings, spouses, friends, colleagues that did not come true.
- Assumption about investment that went wrong.
- Assumption that the movie or the tennis match will be interesting, but it turned out to be otherwise. In general, assumption of an event that occurred in a manner contrary to what you expected.

Steps to not becoming unhappy due to expectations and assumptions:

- Understand that we see the reality not as the reality is. We see the reality with the lenses of our assumptions and expectations. If the reality is making you unhappy, you may examine your own lenses of assumptions and expectations.

- It is fine to have assumptions and expectations. Why should the event always unfold the way one wants? Should one remain prepared for what happens?
- Always ask, "What good has happened even if the things did not happen as per my expectation?"
- Develop ability to see things from different perspectives.
- Develop the flexibility to accept reality the way it happens.
- Minimize expectations.
- Make more refined and calculated assumptions.

It is important to understand that our expectations and assumptions can make us happy or unhappy. So, if you are not happy due to any event, just check if the assumptions and expectations are not the reasons. Once you understand this, you may adjust them as per the need.

PART III

DEEP ACTION TOOLS

CHAPTER 10

Health and Lifestyle

"Healthy body keeps healthy mind."

—Proverb

Health, physical conditions, and lifestyle influence the state of mind and eventually emotions, moods, and feelings. In this chapter, the goal is to make you aware of the things you may want to keep in mind, know more, and follow up on after reading this chapter.

Health:

- At the extreme end of the spectrum, we observe that if someone is suffering from any serious disease, his emotions and moods may swing toward negativity. Going through surgery, recovering from multiple fractures, coping with chronic gastrointestinal problems, or any serious allergy are some of the examples.

- At the lighter end of the spectrum, if someone is tired, has done extreme physical work, is sleep deprived, has excessive food or no food, excessive alcohol, they may have negative moods and less control over emotions and moods.
- On the other end of the spectrum, someone who is healthy, who has proper food habits, exercise and physical activity plans, with proper amount of sleep, etc. will have more control over his emotions and moods.

Physical Conditions:

- Long-term conditions: If you are surrounded by a polluted environment, a noisy neighborhood, unhygienic water sources, you are more likely to feel negative.
- Temporary conditions: If you are visiting a place that has noise due to ongoing celebrations or you are on a tour and end up in a place that has less hygienic conditions, it can influence your mind.

Lifestyle:

- If you are a chronic alcoholic, irregular with food intake and sleep, you may end up unhealthy.
- If you have a sedentary lifestyle and you are less active physically, you may develop obesity.
- If you are regular in exercise or physical activities, you will be healthy.
- If you practice prayer, meditation, or mindfulness, regularly take vacation time out of your busy work life, you are more likely to maintain stability of mind.

The following is a list of things you want to keep in mind for proper health.

1. Healthy Food Habits (right food at right time in right amount)
    Things to note/observe/monitor

    -   Calories
    -   Amount of carbohydrates, fats, protein, lipids, vitamins, minerals, and water
    -   Amount of food
    -   Timing of food, starting from breakfast to dinner
    -   Good hygienic habits (cleanliness in kitchen, knowing expiry dates of food, washing hands, etc.)
    -   Amount of food before special activities (e.g., before an exam, before long hiking, etc.)

2. Maintaining Proper Weight

    -   Maintain calorie input in your food appropriately.
    -   Develop muscles that burn more energy compared to fat.
    -   Do regular exercises.

3. Proper Sleep
    Things to note for proper sleep:

    -   Amount of sleep needed depends on individuals and varies according to age. Select the right amount of sleep for you.

- Maintain sleep timing and rhythm.
- Do not drink or eat food that keeps you alert and hinders sleep.
- Create an appropriate environment for sleep.

  - Comfortable bed
  - Noise-free environment
  - Very dim light or no light
  - Proper temperature of the room
  - Keep non-critical electronic/mobile devices on silent mode

- Consult authorized medical personnel for any sleep disorders.

4. Optima Exercise and Physical Activities
   The following are a few activities that may give you required exercise and physical activity:

   - Walking, jogging, running, swimming
   - Aerobic exercises
   - Strength building and muscle building exercises
   - Sports and games
   - Yoga

5. Freedom from addictions: You want to be away from any kind of addictions.

6. Relaxation habits: You may want to have proper relaxation habits. You may have plans for daily activities, weekly activities, monthly activities, or periodic vacation plans.

7. Regular check-ups of vital body parameters: You may want to consult your family physician for regular check-ups of vital body parameters like blood pressure, cholesterol levels, etc. You may go for yearly detailed medical check-ups if it helps you. Prevention is always better than cure.

8. Maintain a hygienic home, office, and neighborhood.

   - Notice expiration dates of food before eating.
   - Wash hands before eating.
   - Control pests in home/office.
   - Clean house/office with liquids that kill germs.
   - Dispose your garbage and trash regularly and properly.
   - Use air refreshers when needed.

9. Get precautionary vaccinations if and when required.

   - Vaccinate the children.
   - Vaccinate on occasion of breakout of any disease.
   - Vaccinate when going for international tours.

10. Keep yourself updated about recent research and development in the field of medicine.

Mind and body are part of only one system. The discussion of mind management is incomplete without this chapter. Please feel free to research more on the health and hygiene-related topics.

CHAPTER 11

Concept of Self

"Know thyself."

—Proverb

Scenario: "Who am I? What is my identity? What is the meaning of my life without my job? How people will see me now? Will they respect me?" Tom was trying to find answers to these questions. He spent a decade as an expert software engineer in a premium company. He was proud of his job and always identified himself with his work, but the recession took away his job. Now, suddenly, he lost that identity. He was in constant turmoil after his layoff. He was depressed.

Comments: Tom was depressed because he identified himself excessively with his work. If he had realized he was much more than just a software expert, he would not be depressed.

Now, let me ask you, "Who are you?" What is your answer? How we identify ourself plays a role in how we experience emotions, moods, anxiety, and even depression.

The goal of this chapter is to create the awareness that we have many choices for identifying ourselves. Due to any reason, if one of the identities is creating problems, we may shift our focus to other identities so that we become more resourceful in handling the situation.

Can we challenge ourselves to identify with the last two categories mentioned here (especially in the time of darkness and difficulties)? Think about this.

Self-identification categories:

Please note that these categories are subjective. You can categorize self-identity in different ways. Our goal here is to establish a platform for knowing the self. Please note that all of the following categories are part of our lives. We may want to develop flexibility to focus on the right identity that makes our life situation better.

So, let us explore each one of them and discuss when and how our focus on these identities can make our life happy or unhappy.

(1) Self-identity with birth, name, body characteristics, family background, ethnicity, culture, country:

- Name: All of us have a name. Do you like your first name and the last name? Or do you dislike any one of them? Well, now you know that it is just one aspect of your identity.

- Body and its characteristics: If we had an option before our birth to choose which body we preferred to have, we might have chosen a different body or we might chose the one we have. Maybe, if given an option, we can adjust and fine-tune some features of our body. But now, we need to accept it. Well, we may change some aspect of it, like our weight.

    o Difficult situations: Sometimes, a person may have some congenial disorders. Someone might have a disease that changes a body part. Or someone might have lost a body part in an accident. This can lead us to unhappiness and depression. Well, we may want to do the best to recover from any difficulty. At the end, we need to remember that this is not the only identity we have.

- Family background: What is your family background? Do you like it or dislike it? If you like it, it is good for you. If you don't like any of its aspects, let's not focus on it. There is little we can do to change it. So, we may choose to focus forward in a positive way.

- Ethnicity, culture, country, and geographic location: We all have our identification with all these categories. Make sure if something goes wrong, it does not control your mind in a negative way.

Take-home message: If you are the lucky one that is happy with all the identity traits that are connected to your birth, then there is nothing to worry about for you. Make sure that you do not become egoistical or overconfident if you are from a strong background. On the other hand, if you don't like any of the part of this identity, find out if there is anything that you can do to change. And remember, this is just one aspect of your identity. It should not control your mind.

(2) Self-identification with possessions:
We may identify with the house we own, the farm we have, the vehicle, money, wealth, pets, etc. we have. Make sure you don't become arrogant for having something. If you lose something, you may become depressed or sad. I might be a millionaire today, and what if I lose the money due to any reason? Does this mean the end of my life? Possessions may come and go. Life moves on. If any possession or its loss is making you either excessively proud or unhappy, you may want to shift your focus of identity.

(3) Self-identification with others' opinions:
Many times, we give unnecessary importance to others' opinion about us. Well, all healthy feedback, advice, and guidance are welcome, but when we pay attention to others' opinion in excess, we end up giving the remote control of our emotions, feelings, and moods in others' hands.

Are we living to make "only" other people happy? I think it is not the case. We need not depend on others' opinions for self-identity.

(4) Self-identifications with capabilities:
What specific capabilities do you have? Are you good at sports, in arts, in study, in music, in cooking, in hiking, in acting, in dancing, and the list would go on and on? We should be decently proud of our capabilities. If our capability is not giving us the result we need, it is OK. For example, you might be good at picking the right stocks, but due to the upheavals recently in the economy, if your judgments are not giving you optimum results, there is no need to feel sad and depressed. If you are a sportsman and this season was not good for you, it is fine. Many great sports legends have gone through rough times. The point is if you are over-bonded with your capability as your identity and if things go wrong, it will hurt you more. So shift the focus of identity whenever necessary.

(5) Self-identification with disposition and personality:
What is your nature? How is your personality? What happens if people criticize any one of them? Assume that you are a thoughtful and careful decision-maker. If someone is a fast decision-maker, he may criticize you for your relatively slow decision-making habits. Do you want to feel bad about it? A person of

one personality trend may criticize a different personality. This should not make you feel sad.

(6) Self-identification with education, job, or career:
We discussed the case of Tom at the beginning of this chapter. If he is too much identified with his job, losing the job may hurt him more. We are all proud of our education, job, and career. We should be happy about it up to the right degree, and any criticism or loss should not control our mind.

(7) Self-identification with relationships:
Jenifer was devastated. She thought her world ended with her divorce. It was painful for her to end the relationship of five years and move on in life. She never expected this day would come in her life. She had completely identified herself with her relationship. And now she was finding it difficult to recover. We have many more individuals to share love and care. Of course, all relations are significant aspects of our life, but any unwanted turns in it should not take away the controls from our mind.

(8) Self-identification with life situations:
Life situations can be good or bad. You might have achieved something significant. This achievement should not make you egoistic. At the same time, you might be going through a miserable situation. It is all part of life.

(9) Self-identification with belief systems:
We may have a belief system and we may get identified with it. Our belief system may depend upon our family background, culture, our experiences, or any other factors.

(10) Self-identification with consciousness (or life):
If you are reading this book, you are alive. There is a consciousness that makes you different compared to a stone. This is also our identity. We are conscious human beings. Compared to inanimate forms of matter, we are in a better position to live this life. There are the roaring oceans, the magnificent mountains, and the powerful atmospheric system. We have constructed tall buildings, airplanes, satellites, submarines, vehicles, electronics, and computers. All these things are magnificent, but we are different and unique compared to them. We are aware of our self. We can experience pain and pleasure. We can enjoy a beautiful rainbow, melodious music, delicious food, and the fragrance of flowers. Let us realize this and take this opportunity to live the best life we can. Let this consciousness be our ultimate identity.

(11) Self-identification with our place in the universe:
We live in a humungous universe. The universe is full of wonders. One of the wonders is human life. It has taken the universe a few billion years to create this body. Just imagine how capable this body is. The body makes sure that the energy and oxygen reaches each and every cell without our

active participation. When we are hurt and bleed, the body knows how to clot the blood without our active intervention. Our body is a wonderful entity. Many elements that make our body were formed in previous generations of stars. Those gigantic stars exploded at the end of their life cycle, and these elements were scattered into the universe before our solar system was formed. We are in a true sense a cosmic phenomenon. How about human consciousness? How about human capabilities? There are millions of species of living beings on this earth, and only we have the capability to read, write, appreciate art, music, literature, and study science. We are a significant part of this universe. We are products of a few billions of years of the development of this universe. Let us remember this. Let us appreciate this.

What we learned in this section? We have many options for self-identity. If any specific thing is bothering you, gain the flexibility to move to another identity and be happy. Make sure you spend some time contemplating the last two identities mentioned here.

> The body begins with a single cell.
> That one cell becomes mighty bones.
> The pumping heart and thinking brain
> All come out of that single cell.

> That thinking brain can learn language.
> It comprehends science and logic.
> Art, literature, and music
> All come from that ingenious brain.

There are thousands of living species.
Only we are gifted with such a capable brain.
We might have done miracles.
The biggest miracle is our own self.

Only we can wonder at the stars and the moon
And ponder about life and death.
This is a wonderful opportunity.
Let us make the best of our own self.

CHAPTER 12

Purpose of Life

*Our personality modulates with
the purpose of our life.*

A few decades back, a young ambitious Californian founded a computer company. After a few years, that company fired him. For an ordinary man, this would be a big bite to swallow, but this young man had a clear purpose in his life. He wanted to leave behind a dent in the universe. So the toughest situation did not break him down. He continued his life of creativity and innovation. Eventually, the company hired him back and the rest is history. Yes, he was Steve Jobs.

Understanding the purpose of life, the goal of life, the concept of life, and the meaning of life gives us a big picture to focus on when we are going through tough times. Let us discuss some of the purposes/meanings/goals of life and put them in reference with all living beings. You may realize that many of these purposes are true at the right time in the right reference. This will give you an opportunity to explore them and have the awareness to choose what suits the best for a given situation. You may add other purposes of life as per your choice or requirement.

1. Life is to eat, drink, and enjoy:
    We can't live without eating and drinking. However, we may not limit our life to just eating, drinking, and enjoying. Let us see which other life forms also share this purpose. The microorganisms, insects, the aquatic and marine life forms, plants, birds, animals, and humans all eat, drink, and extend their species. They might eat and drink differently, but they consume something for energy. To gain a perspective, if this is our only life goal, we are living life with similar purposes as those the above-mentioned living beings have. Our form of life can have diverse purposes as well, which we may want to explore.

2. Life is to accumulate wealth:
    Let us include various types of wealth forms— financial wealth, political power, social fame, and any other wealth you want for our discussion. Many animals store food in their body as fat. Many plants and insects have their own way of storing the essentials for life. We also need to make sure we store life essentials. Humans have gone one step further compared to other living beings. We developed economy and invented money. Now, we can trade money for water and food as well as many life essentials. It is essential to

fulfill the basic needs of survival. Financial wealth can help us. So, we need to have enough money. The logic is good so far. What happens when we forget the basic reason behind having money and become obsessive about accumulating money only? What happens when accumulating money becomes the purpose of our life? What do you think? How will our life be different compared to other living beings?

Let us explore political power. Many insects and animals have hierarchies in their small societies. Many of them focus on being on the top of those hierarchies for a long time. We have developed sophisticated systems of politics and hierarchy in business units. Power is useful and political systems make our life efficient in many ways. The question arises when we forget the reason behind the political system and end up considering the purpose of life as gaining power. If the life purpose remains only to become powerful, how are we different compared to other living beings? Where is "humanness" in our life?

3. Life is dedicated for one of the "self-identities" mentioned in the previous chapter:
    Many times, we dedicate our life for one of our identities. For example, one may dedicate his/her life for a family member who is in need. One may dedicate one's life for the improvement of the community we belong to, to the society of which we are a part, and many other reasons. As far as the "self-identity" is concerned, we are working

for personal betterment along with others. In this kind of life purposes, we have a few similarities and many differences compared to other life forms. Humans have well-developed emotions, developed sociopolitical structures, and value systems compared to other life forms. Here, the things differ compared to other life forms.

4. Life is dedicated to unselfish endeavors:
   An individual may dedicate life for the betterment of community, society, and human beings in need or for any other good cause. I don't think there is any other life form that can live such a life. In this way of living, we are different from other life forms mentioned. I believe this is a uniquely human endeavor.

5. Life is to bring out the best quality in us:
   We may have special talents. Some of us are good at one or more qualities, like painting, singing, music, acting, cooking, writing, poetry, teaching, education, research, mentoring, sports, athletics, any specific hobby, and many more such abilities. One may decide to dedicate life to the pursuit of such an endeavor and utilize the best resources we have. The pursuit may also include and not be limited to financial gain from our ability, social fame, satisfaction of living life, etc. Where do we stand if this is our purpose of life compared to other life forms starting from microorganisms to animals? Well, I am not aware of any other living forms pursuing such activities. The pursuit of such qualities is found only in humans. So, in this case,

we are doing something different compared to other life forms.

6. Life is the quest to find the ultimate truth of existence and consciousness:
   Many of us spend our lives in search of the ultimate truth and purpose of life. Why does this universe exist? How did it come in to existence? Was there any beginning and how was it? How did life begin? Is the Earth the only planet with life? Who am I? Where was I before I was born? What will happen to me after death? Why do the laws of science exist? Who made these laws? Is there a God, and if yes, who and how is he? Many of us study science to find such answers. Many take philosophical and spiritual routes in search of truth. I think this is a uniquely human endeavor. No other life form has demonstrated such extensive search for the meaning of their existence.

7. Life is to have balance of many of the above purposes: We may take a balanced approach. We may decide that we want to focus on all the above-mentioned aspects in the right amount. This "right amount" varies from person to person. We want to enjoy food, we want to earn wealth, have power as and when needed, care for our identities—family, friend, community, etc., want to spend some time for unselfish charity work, bring out the best in us at the right time, and pursue the quest for the meaning of life. Yes, this is also an approach that many of us take. This is quite unique for humans only.

A few points to ponder about:

In addition to the above-mentioned life purposes and goals, the following are a few points worth contemplating:

- Life compared to many other people in the world: If I look at today's world, I see many humans suffering from poverty. I see people do not have the same opportunity for education and infrastructure. There are people who do not have primary education and do not have the ability to explore resources like the Internet. These people are also living their best possible lives.

  On the other hand, when we have small problems compared to the above-mentioned situations, we become unhappy. It is fine to be unhappy for some short amount of time, but we need to appreciate all that we have. We need to put ourselves in the global perspective and be grateful for what we have. Let us not get disturbed by relatively small problems. Let us live our life to the fullest.

- Bigger perspective of life:
  Adversities come and go; life moves on. Life, which gives me the potential of happy moments, is always here. Why not appreciate life itself? Why not realize that if I am conscious, I can be happy? Why not understand that life is a gift that nature has given us? Where would I go to complain if I was not created or I did not

come to existence? My very existence gives me an opportunity to experience the wonders of this life. My very life gives me an opportunity to experience love and friendship. My life gives me an opportunity to pursue what I like. So why not focus on the big picture? Why focus on trivial things and become unhappy? No one has lived a perfect life. Everyone has experienced failure in one or another form. I also have my unhappy days, but how can some small things control my mind, my emotions, and my thoughts and make me unhappy for a long time? Let me realize this. Let me take charge of my own mind; let me live positively hereafter.

- Life from the view of progressive improvement in maturity:

  A child cries for a toy. We all know that the child is immature, and for him, toys are his world. If a toy is broken, he thinks his world is broken. The child becomes an adult. Now, he will not cry for those toys. Why? Because adults understand that toys are not the only goals of life.

  Now, this adult will cry for other things. Now, he will cry for money, relationships, power, etc. If you think carefully, can you visualize that the adult has just changed his toys? Now, the toys are defined in different ways. But if we really understand who we are in a deeper sense and what the purpose of life is, these small things should also not bother us for a long time.

Can we transcend to a higher level of maturity of life such that small things do not trouble us? Understanding the consciousness and universe, can't we mature to one more level and not get disturbed by the very things that bother us now? Contemplate on this.

CHAPTER 13

Programmed and Conditioned Mind

*Our programmed and conditioned mind influences
the way we see and interpret the world.*

Let us do this thought experiment. Consider a baby boy of
age about two to three years. Give him two choices. The
first choice is the box of chocolates he loves. The second
choice is a dinner date with Miss Universe. Which of the
two choices do you think he would select? I bet he will go
for the first one—the box of chocolates he loves.

Now, fast forward twenty years and give him the same
two choices. Which do you think he would select? I
bet, in most of the cases, he would select the second
one—the dinner date with Miss Universe. Why? Well,
it is natural for a young man of twenty-three years to get
attracted toward a beautiful young lady. This is how we are
"conditioned" or "programmed" biologically. Our body has
certain characteristics. These characteristics make us react
to things in a particular way. In an adult male body, there

will be a natural attraction toward beautiful young females. Any living species that does not have male and female classification (like bacteria) may not have such attractions. The point is, knowingly or unknowingly, we respond to the given situation biased by the biology we live with. This is what I would call "biological programming."

I am using the word "programming" from the familiar world of computers. When we enter a program in a computer, the computer executes it. Biological programming has a similar effect. However, there is a difference as well. While a computer has no choice but to execute the program, humans have choice. If we understand the origin of the response, we can modify and control the response. In the above example, if a young man has affection for the young woman, how the man behaves is in his hands. If we become aware of our programming, we can improve our reactions and responses. This is the focus of this chapter.

What is the point in discussing the "conditioning" or "programming" when we are talking about managing the mind? Well, we need to understand that many of our emotional reactions are based on deeper programs and a conditioned mind. We live under the influences of many conditionings. The body we have has its own biology, which influences the emotions, feelings, moods, etc. The culture and society we live in have their conditioning. Our own experiences also condition us. If we understand this programming and conditioning, it will help us gain superior control over our mind and over our emotions, feelings, moods, and stress.

Let us discuss the possible programming and conditioning we may have and how they help us understand our emotions, moods, and feelings.

- Biological programming: Emotions have biological roots. Our brain parts, like the amygdala, are involved in emotional responses. We are biologically programmed for the survival response when we see a threat to our existence. In addition to basic emotions like fear and anger, our biology influences our mind in many activities. It gives us a signal of hunger, thirst, etc. Our biology needs sleep, and any disturbance in sleep can also cause irritation. When we are sick, biology changes and the state of mind is influenced. In summary, if we understand this, we may start taking appropriate actions when needed.

- Cultural/Social conditioning and programming: Every culture and society has its own flavor of living. In fact, every family has its own culture. When we interact with people from different backgrounds, we need to understand that many of the things in their behavior are due to the differences in cultural and social backgrounds. There are many ways to do one thing. Here, the question is not about right or wrong. We need not become judgmental about others.

  When things do not meet our expectations, we may become unhappy. The point is many times, our unhappiness is caused due to our expectations that need not be universally followed. If we understand this, we may handle our mind more effectively. The following are some aspects that differ among cultures that may cause irritation or unhappiness in us.

o   The way each culture greets when we meet is different.
o   In many cultures, looking into the eyes while talking can be a sign of attention given to the other person. In many cultures, people do not look into the eyes directly as a gesture of respect.
o   Many people communicate directly. For example, people say "no" directly if they disagree. In other cultures, people take an indirect approach of saying "no." For example—they delay the decision.
o   The dining manners are different in different cultures.
o   Feel free to list more things from your own observations.

•   Experiential conditioning and programming: Most of us learn from our experiences. The experiences can be good or bad. Learning is essential and useful. If we are successful in one of our goals, we may want to repeat the approach we took to achieve other endeavors. Sometimes, we may generalize things. If we have gone through a bad experience, we may want to avoid it another time. From our experience, we prepare a model of the world. We conclude—"This is the way the world is." We need to become aware and realize that we are reacting as per our model of the world. The world is not bound to follow our model. When the world does not follow our model, we may become unhappy, irritated, sad, etc. If we understand this, we may manage our mind efficiently. The following are examples of some of the conclusions we draw from our experiences.

o   People are selfish. There must be some hidden strings in all lucrative offers.
o   Never trust certain types of people.
o   I need not pay more than a certain amount for this specific service.
o   Please add a few more of your own observations.

•   Beliefs: We all have our beliefs. Many times, they are useful. Once in a while, we end up with the beliefs that limit us and make us unhappy. We may believe that "I should never fail." And if I fail, it makes me sad. I might have a philosophy that everything I do must be perfect. Now, by any chance, if something imperfect happens through my efforts, I might be unhappy. The following are some of the beliefs we may have. Please note that many of such beliefs might be personal and others may not follow them. Understanding that we are looking at the world through the glasses of our beliefs make us more flexible when things do not follow our way of thinking.

o   Everyone should respect me.
o   I am always right.
o   I know more.

o   No one can progress more than I have if they also come from the similar background I have come from. I am great.

o   My culture, community, country is the best

o   If I let go, I appear weak.

o   If I am strong, I must dominate.

o   Please add some more beliefs from your observations.

What is the take home message from this chapter? Well, we all have conditioned minds and programmed responses. If we understand this, we may become more flexible.

When we want to manage emotions, feelings, and moods of other individuals, we must understand their background. We should identify conditioning due to their social, cultural, experience background and their belief systems. This knowledge will make us more capable to understand others and help them manage their state of mind.

CHAPTER 14

Meditation

*When I meditate, I feel deeply
connected with existence.*

When we meditate, we are in touch with existence. We understand our inner self in a much richer sense. We are calm, relaxed, and free of tensions. There are many benefits of meditation. The positive effects of meditation are observed in the long term. If you meditate once or just a few times, you may not get the full benefit. The mind is trained gradually. So let us begin our voyage of meditation.

The word "meditation" is used in several ways. In normal language, to meditate means to think, contemplate, and reflect. When I use the word meditation, I do *not* mean thinking or contemplation.

Meditation is also not concentration. For me, concentration means focus. If I am reading, I want to focus only on reading. I don't want to get disturbed by the surrounding sounds. Concentration is needed in life. It has its own applications. For me, meditation is not limited to focusing on one thing. Meditation means living in the "here and now" with total awareness. In the beginning, we may use one tool as an anchor that can keep us in the "here and now". The goal is to be aware of everything else as well, without being judgmental. Of course, we care about our safety and take right action if required.

There is one more term—mindfulness. This term is very close in meaning to how I describe the term "meditation." Different traditions use different words. I prefer the word "meditation."

How can we meditate? The simplest thing is to bring one's attention to the present moment and present place. Our mind is very agile. It digs into past memories and projects the future. So we need different "anchors" to keep ourselves in the "here and now."

When we are in a meditative state, there is no worry and no anxiety. Our mind is relaxed. Here are two of many reasons why we experience calmness and serenity. The first is we accept everything without being judgmental. Secondly, there is no worry if our mind is in the present.

I heard a Zen story. Please note that the stories have many versions. You might have heard a different version.

A man was followed by a lion in a deep forest. To save himself, he ran fast. The lion was gradually catching up with him. In a moment of chaos, the man's leg slipped and he fell into a valley. He managed to catch a branch of a tree while rolling down the hill. He looked up, and the lion was waiting for him. He looked down and he saw a deep valley. Somehow, he was hanging there with the support of a very thin branch of the tree. Then he saw two mice cutting the branch he was hanging on. The branch was so thin that if they cut a bit more, he would fall into the valley. At that moment, he saw a strawberry hanging on the adjacent branch. He managed to grab the strawberry and ate it.

"This is the most delicious strawberry I have ever eaten!" he exclaimed.

If we live moment to moment, we may enjoy every moment. Life might be very difficult. We might be in the midst of turmoil in our life. Yes, we accept that turmoil. We do the best to come out of the turmoil. While working hard to manage the situation, can we become calm inside? Can we take out time for meditation in which we promise ourselves that we will remain in the present?

I have been practicing meditation for about twenty years. I have explored various methods of meditation. The following are my ten favorite methods of meditation. I suggest you experiment with one at a time and find out your favorite. If you like more than one method, you may use any one when you want.

Before I discuss the ten methods, let me summarize the attributes of meditation.

- Total presence in "here and now"
- Total acceptance without judgments (Note: maintain safety)

- Observe thoughts in mind without criticism, just be a witness
- Use one anchor to remain in "here and now"
- Remain aware of surroundings

Where and when to meditate?

- Find a safe place.
- Find a place where you encounter minimum disturbance in your activity.
- Wear comfortable clothes.
- Put all personal mobile devices on silent mode.
- Choose any time of the day convenient for you.
- Determine the amount of time you will meditate. You may use a timer or alarm to count minutes. Start with short time periods.

Now, let us begin the discussion on the meditations.

Method 1: Meditate on breathing.

Sit down or lie down comfortably. Relax. Breathe normally. There might be some sound or some smell. Acknowledge and accept the surroundings. Observe how your body feels on a chair or on a mattress. Observe if there is any discomfort in your body. Adjust the body position and relax. You may close your eyes if it minimizes distraction.

Now, gradually, observe your breathing. Observe if the incoming breath is warm or cold. Observe how it touches your nostrils. You may hear a subtle sound when the breath passes through the nostrils, then throat. The air then goes toward the lungs. Notice how the abdomen expands. You can feel that movement. The abdomen stops expanding and starts contracting. The breathe-out cycle begins. You may notice the abdomen coming down. You may notice the breath coming out from your lungs through the throat and touching the nostrils. There is a subtle sound when the air touches the nostrils. You may feel this air a bit warmer. Once you exhale the air completely, the abdomen stops moving. A new cycle begins.

Observe the cycles of breath. Pay attention. At the same time, be aware of the surroundings. There might be sounds of a second hand of a clock, any bird, or humans outside your room. Just witness any sound that you hear. Notice if the body feels any tension. Adjust if needed.

Start with five minutes of daily meditation. Practice regularly. Decide the time for daily practice. After a few days, you may increase the time duration.

Method 2: Meditate on the pauses between breathing cycles.

Sit down or lie down comfortably and relax. Breathe normally. Accept all surrounding sounds. First, observe the complete breathing cycles.

Observe the incoming breath. The air touches the nostrils and then passes through the throat into the lungs. Your abdomen expands during breathing in. Then, for a fraction of a second, the abdomen stops. There is no movement of body for this fraction of the second. There is no movement of air either. There is a pause between incoming breath and outgoing breath. Observe this pause. It is a very small time period. Just remain witness to this moment when the breath pauses.

The breathe-out cycle begins. You may notice the air coming out from the lungs through the throat and then the nostrils. Once the air is out, the breathing stops. There is no movement of the abdomen for a fraction of a second. Observe this moment. This is the moment of pause between the breathe-out cycle and the new breathe-in cycle.

In this method, your attention should be on the pauses. Make sure you do not stretch the time of pause intentionally. This time period is very short, may be just a second or less. This time may vary from person to person. You need to be very normal. Your complete attention should be on those two points in the breathing cycle. Just notice those pauses and come in contact with the "here and now."

Method 3: Meditate by looking at an object.

Choose an object for which you have positive feelings like respect, devotion, etc. It is essential that you select the object that neither induces any imagination of any kind nor the memory recall of any type. You may choose a statue or a photo of someone you worship. It can be a small plant, a flower, or a pebble. Focus on this object will be the anchor for you to remain in the "here and now."

Sit down in a relaxed position. Put the object before you such that you can see it comfortably. Relax. You need to see it in a normal way. Blink your eyes normally. Be aware of the blinking on a regular basis. Notice if there is any sound or smell. Witness the surroundings and accept everything it has.

Now, start looking at the object and think of that object only. Is it three-dimensional or flat? You may observe its shape, details of parts, color, shades of colors, brightness, size, position with reference to you, etc. Be completely aware of the surrounding. Be aware of your thoughts. Whenever the mind goes to past or future, bring back the concentration to the object.

If you wish, you may close your eyes briefly. When eyes are closed, just be aware of surrounding sounds and smells if any. Feel your body and observe how comfortable it is. Whenever the mind starts wandering, look at the object and anchor yourself in the present. Be relaxed, calm, and peaceful.

Method 4: Meditate on nature.

Have you observed a sense of calmness when you visit a mountain resort, walk through woods, wander on a seashore, or just look at a beautiful sunset? This is a glimpse of the meditation that one gets at natural places.

Where does one find such "natural places" in everyday life? Consider the following:

- Look at the sky during sunrise or sunset.
- Go to a park full of colorful flowers and plants.
- Go to a seashore or river bank if any one of them is near your residence.
- Look at the flowers and trees in your personal garden.
- Look at the clouds and rain when it is raining. Listen to the sound of thunder.

On weekends or short vacations, you may go to any natural place of your choice.

How should you meditate once you pick your natural place? You may sit down comfortably or you may walk slowly. Observe all sensory inputs. Start with vision. Observe the beauty of nature. Observe the colors, shades of colors, brightness, etc. Hear the sounds of birds, water flowing, and wind. Hear the intensity of sound, loudness of the sound, melody of the sound. Feel the surroundings. If you are at the seashore, feel the moist air. Feel the wind on your face. Is it gentle or very fast? Feel the smell of flowers and plants around. Every place has its unique smell. Experience it. Be aware of the surroundings. Just remain with nature in the "here and now".

This meditation involves many variations. For example, walking on the seashore will be different compared to looking at the sky during sunset from the terrace. So, keeping the main principles of meditation in mind, develop your own detailed steps after you select a natural place.

Method 5: Meditate on any activity.

To be in the "here and now" is the goal of meditation. This is possible to achieve even if we are doing any activity.

Consider just walking. You may take a normal walk anytime, anywhere. Suppose you are walking in a garden. Just remain aware of the surroundings. In addition, observe the process of walking: how you lift your right leg; how you move forward; put it on the earth; and lift the left leg. Feel the hardness or the softness of the ground. The hands also move with the legs gently. Observe the harmony in the movement of hands and legs. Observe how your breathing changes with the walking speed. If you are walking fast for a long time, observe the perspiration and the cooling effect it brings on your skin.

You can choose any activity and remain mindful. The following are some activities that you may choose. Be sure you choose the safe activity.

- Consider talking on the phone. Just be aware of how you hold the phone, how you speak and listen. Do you also walk while you talk?

- Consider lunch or dinner. Observe how you prepare your dish, eat the food, and chew it, how it tastes, and how you swallow the food. Observe all the activities.

- Consider reading a book: how the book feels in your hand; how you read. Do you also speak loudly in your mind what you read? Observe all activities.

- Consider writing or typing on the keyboard. Observe how fast your fingers move. Do you speak the words in your head? Do you see the typing on the computer screen? Pay attention to all activities.

- Consider taking a shower. Just observe how the water drops fall on your body. How the gentle falling of water on your face and head can relax you. Be aware of all the activities you do.

- You may try any other activity in which you are comfortable and safe.

Method 6: Meditate on sudden stops in any activity.

Preferably, you want to do this meditation in privacy. Stop any activity suddenly and spontaneously. Of course, please choose activities wisely and be safe. When there is a sudden stop, the mind also stops for a few seconds, and you will experience a deep calmness. All the general attributes of the meditation apply here as well.

Consider just walking in your bedroom. Observe yourself walking and suddenly stop. Become a statue. When you stop suddenly, you will observe high intensity calmness for a few moments after the stop. Once the intensity decreases, walk again. Randomly stop again and become a statue. Observe how the mind stops thinking for a few moments.

You can decide for how long you want to remain as a statue. Make sure that you take the decision of stopping spontaneously. Or you may be helped by a partner in this activity.

Choose the activities that you can do without much effort, like walking, gentle jogging, dancing, eating, etc. Make sure you maintain safety.

Method 7: Meditate on sound.

Choose a melodious sound. Choose a sound that you like, a sound that gives you positive feelings and energy. The following are some candidates for selection.

- Sound of a musical instrument
- Sound of a vowel you speak
- Sound of water drops
- Sound of water flow
- Sound of the second hand of a clock
- Sound of birds
- Sound of rain
- Use recorded sounds of any of the above if needed.

How to meditate? Once you decide the sound, sit comfortably. If you want to stand, stand comfortably. Then, listen to the sound attentively. Listen how the sound begins, how it picks up the volume and intensity, reaches the peak, and then gradually fades away. There might be an interval of no sound, and then the sound begins again. If sound is random and does not repeat, it is fine as well. Observe the quality of the sound, its intensity, volume, loudness, pitch, and changes in it, how far the sound is, etc. Be witness to the sound. In addition to this, be aware of the surroundings; apply all other attributes of meditation.

Method 8: Meditate on taste and smell.

You can involve any positive taste or smell for meditation purposes. The following is a list. You may extend the list as per your preference.

- Drinking tea
- Drinking coffee
- Drinking any fruit juice
- Drinking water
- Smell of flowers
- Smell of sandalwood or any other thing used for devotional purposes

How to do the meditation? Well, by now, you already have the answer. For this activity, preferably sit down comfortably in a quiet place. Take a cup of tea or coffee and drink slowly, gently, and gradually. Observe how it touches the tongue. How is the taste? Is the taste mild or strong? Observe as the tea touches parts of the mouth and rolls down your throat. The taste may fade away. Just observe the absence of the taste. Then take another sip. Repeat the process for the time you have decided. The smell aspect of tea or coffee can accompany its drinking.

For smell, take a flower and feel its fragrance. How does it smell? Is it strong or mild? Is it something you like or not? Does it fade away after some time? Notice all these changes. Keep in mind all other attributes of meditation.

Method 9: Meditate by observing emotions, moods, and feelings.

This meditation can be done at any place. However, in the initial phase of learning, you may want to be in a comfortable place. You may sit down comfortably, take a gentle walk, or if you are home, just lie down. Relax. Then, bring your attention to the emotions, feelings, and moods arising in your mind.

Select any specific emotion. Observe how it arises in the mind. Does it also impact the body and disturb the relaxation? How is your facial expression? Observe the intensity of emotion. Does it bring back any memory or create any imagination? If yes, observe the details. Is there any internal talk going on? Be a witness. Observe every aspect of the emotion. There might be other emotions arising alongside it. Observe these emotions or feelings as well.

Method 10: Meditate by observing thoughts.

This mediation can be done anywhere, but in the initial stage of learning, you may choose a quiet place where you may sit comfortably. Relax.

Now, observe all the thoughts going on in your mind. Just remain witness. Remain non-judgmental. Initially, you may observe a very high frequency of thoughts. After you start paying attention, you may observe the frequency decreases. There might be thoughts like "I am observing my thoughts." This is fine. Observe this thought as well.

Remain conscious of surroundings in a nonjudgmental way. There might be a thought that "I should reduce the thoughts." There might be thoughts that "Now, I am meditating." Observe all these thoughts as well. The mind may want to wander in the past and dream about the future. Just observe the activity of the mind. Do not restrict the mind from going into the past or future. Just remain a detached observer.

Many times, the frequency of thoughts may decrease. The serenity may start flowing in your body. As the thoughts decrease in frequency, the gap between the thoughts may increase. You keep observing these gaps as well. "Now, there is no thought." This can also be a thought. Just observe.

After the right amount of practice, you will start feeling calmness.

We learned that meditation is a process of maintaining the awareness in the present. There are many benefits if we meditate for the long term. There are various methods and anchors that we may use for meditation. Ten such methods are described in this chapter. Choose the method that resonates with you. If you need further help, if there are questions, if any problem arises, or if you want to know more about meditation, feel free to contact an expert in this field.

PART IV

MASTERING EMOTIONAL INTELLIGENCE

CHAPTER 15

Game Plan for Emotional Intelligence

"I don't want to be at the mercy of my emotions. I want to use them, to enjoy them, and to dominate them."

—Oscar Wilde

Let us divide emotional intelligence into the following three action-oriented goals.

A. Recognize emotions in self and others.
B. Manage emotions in self and others.
C. Elicit emotions in self and others.

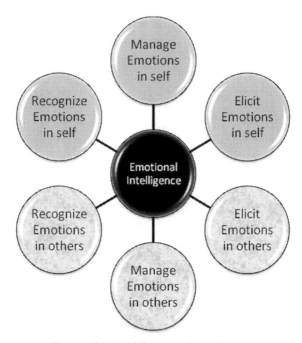

Figure: Goals of Emotional intelligence

Goal A: Recognize emotions in self and others:

To recognize emotions in the self, we need to develop self-awareness. We are aware of our emotions most of the time. Once in a while, the emotional current flows slowly underneath and we may take some time to recognize it.

For recognizing the emotions in others, we need to be observant. We need to understand that another person might have a different social and cultural background and a different belief system. The following activities can help enhance our ability to recognize the emotions in the self and others.

- Improve self-awareness. Observe the thoughts in your mind. Understand how they arise.
- Develop the ability to observe yourself as a third person. If thoughts of happiness are going on in your mind, you should be able to observe that "Thoughts of happiness are going on in my mind."
- Observe patters in personal behavior. You may ask the following questions:

  o Am I getting irritated quickly all the time?
  o Am I developing a pessimistic outlook on life?
  o Is there anything bothering me?
  o Why am I not cheerful most of the time?
  o Am I doing something to prove myself to someone?
  o Is there any recent change in my performance and general behavior?
  o Is there any change in my social or family interaction?

- We may ask similar questions to understand others.
- To recognize emotions in others, we need to develop observational skills and be in the "here and now" to really connect to the other person.
- Understand the paradigm, viewpoints, conditioning, and programming of the other person.

Goal B: Manage the emotions in self and others:

In the previous chapters, we learned two types of tools. The first set was for "Quick Action." The second set was for "Deep Action." Now is the time to develop a strategy using these tools to master the art of managing the emotions.

Let us divide the skill of managing emotions into the following three steps.

1. Accept and acknowledge
2. Examine and analyze
3. Plan and act

Step 1: Accept and acknowledge: We need to accept the situation. We need to identify the emotions that are bothering us. "Yes, I become angry, and I want to have control over my temperament."

"Yes, I am fearful and I need to be realistic about my fears and I want to live normally." Many times, we get into denial mode. We don't accept that a problem exists. Or we don't accept that there is scope for improvement.

Please note that when I say "accept and acknowledge," I don't mean you need to have a public announcement or confession. When I say accept and acknowledge, I mean that you accept things for yourself in your mind. You need not even verbalize it. If it helps to verbalize, do it. For example, if your close friend is working with you to improve the situation, you may accept in his presence. If your mentor or guide is helping you out, you may verbalize the acceptance. If you are making notes and writing a diary, you may write it there for the purpose of improvement.

The following are some limiting thought processes that I observe in people. These thought processes ultimately confine us in an unpleasant state of mind and hinder us from becoming free from them.

- "This is the way life is. I am suffering. There is no way out."
- "Anyone else will do the same in this situation."
- "I have explored all possible ways to come out of my situation. Nothing works. There is no other way left out to try."
- Many times, we identify with miseries. Once we make an unpleasant state our "identity," it is difficult to get out of this state. We may start deriving a sense of self-satisfaction in misery.

If we don't accept the reality, we will never overcome the problem and will never gain mastery. Two things are essential for improving the state of mind. The first is to accept that I am going through an unpleasant state of mind. The second is that there is scope for improvement and I want to sharpen my emotional abilities to have a pleasant state of mind. There can be many more ways to look at the situation. The point is acknowledge that I need to work on the emotions.

Step 2: Examine and analyze:

The second step is to examine and analyze. Let us examine the emotions from two aspects. First is the time and second is intensity.

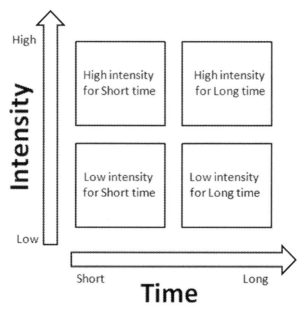

Figure: Examine emotions, feelings, and moods
for two aspects—intensity and time.

Intensity Spectrum: Examine if the intensity of the emotion is low or high. For example, if I am angry, then is the intensity of anger low or high? If I am sad, am I just unhappy or am I dejected and depressed?

Time Spectrum: For how long does the emotion last? If I am angry, does anger fade away with time in a few minutes or is it persistent for several days and weeks? If I am sad, does my sadness last for a few hours or does it last for days and weeks and become depression? Examine the emotions for the duration of the time. When we classify an emotion for a "long" time period, it does not mean that the intensity remains the same for twenty-four hours a day. It means that the emotion comes back frequently with some intensity over a long period of time. One may remember a social insult and become angry frequently with high intensity. The emotion of depression, vengeance, fear can be observed coming back with high intensity over a long time period.

The intensity of emotion may not remain stable, but broadly, for analysis purpose, let us classify the emotions in the following four categories:

- Emotions with low intensity for short time period
- Emotions with high intensity for short time period
- Emotions with low intensity for long time period
- Emotions with high intensity for long time period.

Other analysis: Ask the following questions for detailed analysis.

- What is the root cause of this emotion?
- How can I resolve the root cause? If I can't change the root cause, can I manage the emotions even if the root cause persists?
- Do I need to react emotionally so strongly for the given situation?
- How much importance does this emotion and root cause have in my long vision of life?

Step 3: Plan and act: We have developed two sets of tools. Let us see how they can be implemented.

Quick Action tools: Can be used to decrease the intensity of unwanted emotions and increase the intensity of desired emotions.

Deep Action tools: Can be used to manage emotions that persist over a long period of time.

Let us explore this approach in detail.

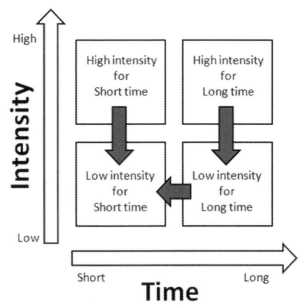

Figure: Action plan to deal with undesired emotions, feelings, and moods

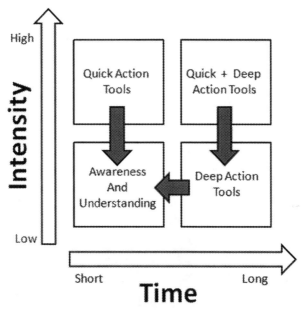

Figure: Use of tool sets to deal with unwanted emotions, feelings, and moods

- For unwanted emotions like anger and sadness, the following can be an action plan.
- Use any of the "Quick Action" tools and decrease the intensity.
- Use "Deep Action" tools and reduce the time of the unwanted emotion.
- Once the emotion has low intensity and arises for a short time, we may easily deal with it through understanding and awareness.

Goal C: Elicit the emotions in self and others:

What state of mind do I want to be in when I am facing a critical situation, like a job interview, a public speech or presentation, or dealing with crisis in a personal relationship? Well, in this situation, I want to have mental calmness, confidence, positive state of mind, and many more positive emotions, feelings, and moods. How can I bring out the desired emotion in myself as and when required? This is the third aspect of emotional intelligence.

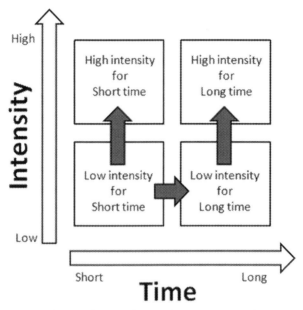

Figure: Action plan to elicit positive and
desired emotions, feelings, and moods

- For desired emotions like happiness, the following can be an action plan.
- Use the "Deep Action" tools so that the good emotion lasts for a long time.
- On required basis, use "Quick Action" tools to increase the intensity.

Where and when do we need positive emotions, feelings, or moods for a long time with high intensity? The following is a possible list of situations. Please add your viewpoints on this as well.

- If you are going through a rough time in a personal relationship, you need to maintain positive emotions, optimism, positive feelings, for a long time with the appropriate intensity.
- If you are facing a career crisis, you need a feeling of self-confidence, optimism, peacefulness of mind, perseverance, and many positive emotions, feelings, moods for a long time.
- If you are going through a difficult medical condition,
- If you are preparing for an exam or competition and the preparation time is long,
- If you are an entrepreneur starting a new project,
- If you are an artist, athlete, actor, writer, innovator, or aiming for any special achievements,
- And even in normal life, many of us have at some time gone through difficulties when we face some kind of failure, in all these situations, we need to have positive emotions, feelings, and moods for a long time with the appropriate intensity.

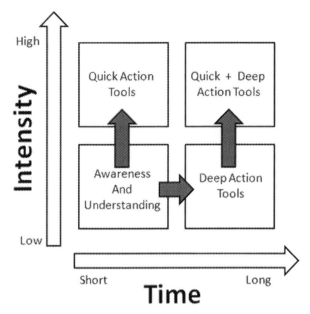

Figure: Use of tool sets to elicit positive and
desired emotions, feelings, and moods

Where do we need positive emotions, feelings, or moods
for a short time but with high intensity?

- Communicating in difficult times in a personal
  relationship, career, or at social situations
- Facing an interview
- Appearing for an exam
- If you are a sportsman, during the time of a game
- If you are an artist, actor, public speaker, you need
  positive attributes at the time of your performance
- If you are going through unanticipated situations,
  like sudden health problems, accident, etc.
- There are many more occasions that you may
  identify.

To elicit the desired emotions in self, the "Quick Action" tools can be useful. Consider the following two examples.

Example 1: I am going to an interview, but I am nervous. I need to have a positive state of mind, calmness of thought, confidence, optimism, and clarity in expressing my thoughts. How can I achieve this? Well, first of all, I use "Deep Action" tools to gain a broader perspective of life. The broader and bigger perspective in a way enhances calmness. It gives the mind stability. Then, I look into the "Quick Action" tools. I use "Memory Recall" and remember the situations of my life where I have faced such situations successfully. Everyone has achieved some success at some point in time. The memory of the success can enhance confidence. During an interview, I may maintain a relaxed body posture, deep breathing, and positive internal talks.

Example 2: I am facing a crisis in a personal relationship. I need to communicate properly, handle the situation calmly. So when I am going for the discussion to resolve the crisis, I can use my "Memory Recall" tool and look back in my life where I have faced such situations successfully. Recalling the successful memory may bring out the emotions that equip me for the current situation. I may use deep breathing techniques to make sure I maintain my calmness. I may maintain relaxed body posture, maintain positive internal talk, relax my expectation, check my assumptions, and remain in the "here and now." I may use "Deep Action" tools to gain the broader vision of life.

The following are some of the questions I may ask myself and others to gain the desired mental state.

- What kind of mental state do I want to achieve in a given situation?
- Which of the "Deep Action" and "Quick Action" tools can help me achieve the desired state?
- I may look back into my "tools" and pick the right tool and implement.
- I may help others to develop such tools.
- I may talk with the other person and build his or her tools as and when required.

A few notes on "eliciting emotions in others":

When we want to elicit emotions in others, the following points should be kept in mind.

- Gain trust. If the other person trusts you, if he is convinced that what you are doing is for his betterment, only then will he follow you.
- There is a saying that actions speak louder than words. If we extend this saying, we may say that a person's character speaks louder than his actions. Make sure that you have the character that other person can rely upon.
- Understand others' viewpoints, situations, cause of emotions/feelings/moods. Acknowledge the situation. Connect to his current state of mind. From there, bring him out gradually using the tools we have discussed.

In summary, we may plan strategically to classify the emotions over time and intensity spectrum, use appropriate tools, and enhance emotional intelligence, manage feelings and moods in self and others.

CHAPTER 16

Sadness

It is human to become sad. It is disease to become depressed. Cure the disease at the earliest.

What causes sadness? Let us imagine a few possible life situations that can make one sad.

I was sad when I came to know about the health of Mark's father. Mark was in deep sorrow as the doctor told him his father was in the last stages of cancer and would survive for only another two months. His grief intensified and he needed my support to walk through this situation. After his father's death, all of his family was in deep mourning. It was a big loss for Mark, as his father was his best friend, his guide, his mentor, and his idol. He was dejected. He suffered a brief period of depression before he recovered from his loss.

Alice was unhappy with the way her relationship was going with Jeff. She was disappointed with Jeff's attitude toward her. She had tried hard to save their two-year long marriage, but now it was moving toward divorce. She was dejected to realize all her dreams about their married life were shattering. Jeff did not care to rebuild the relationship. Alice was gradually drifting toward depression, as she was not able to revive the relationship. Many of Alice's close friends were sad to know she was going through the misery.

The stock market crash was a horrible nightmare come true for Tom. He had saved money over time and invested in stocks. When the economy started declining, he was worried and sad. As time passed by, he was disappointed, as he was seeing his entire asset melting, but he could not do much. He hoped that the economy would recover soon, but things happened for which he was not prepared. His sadness soon turned into grief and dejection as the economy crashed. He was brave. He was doing his best to come out of the miserable situation.

How does one handle "sadness?"

Step 1: Acknowledge and accept: Sadness comes in many forms and names. Here are a few words that describe this emotion with different intensity and context. Let us review them.

Sadness	unhappiness	sorrow	misery	melancholy
Grief	dejection	depression	agony	disappointment

So, if you are going through any of the above emotional states, first acknowledge and accept. This will open the door to change the situation.

Step 2: Examine and analyze:

Let us examine and analyze the following aspects.

- The root cause of the emotion: This will throw light on understanding the situation.
- Intensity and time: We had discussed this in detail in the previous chapters. Understanding this aspect will help us to use the right tools.

The following are a few possible reasons for sadness. The purpose is to think with you and put forward your reasons for sadness. Once we identify the reason, we may do further analysis.

Some possible causes of sadness are:

- Food/traveling/movie/trip/or any minor aspect is not as good as expected.
- Favorite sports team loses a match
- Altercation with spouse/parents/boyfriend/girlfriend that we wish should not have happened

- Strong disagreement with colleague/boss/friend that we wish should not have happened
- Unexpected insult from someone
- Failure in some aspect of life
- Death of loved one
- Divorce or difficult relationships
- Layoff or major financial setback
- Dissatisfied aspects of life (like job, relationship, achievements, etc.)
- Minor/major injury or health problems of self/family/friend
- Please add other possible causes here.
- _____
- _____
- _____

Questionnaire: A few questions you may want to ponder about the current state of emotion.

A. Do I want to remain in this state?
B. Can I change what has happened (like the death of a loved one, divorce, layoff, etc.)?
C. Why should I let this emotion control me?
D. What is the meaning of my life? Why am I stuck in this situation?
E. Why am I not finding the best possible way to live a normal life?
F. What will happen if I remain in this state? The answer can be—no improvement in my mental state, my future life, my family happiness, etc. Do I want this to happen?

G. What will not happen if I remain in this state? Example—I may not focus again on career, studies, relationship, etc. Do I want this to happen?

H. Which activity will get me out of this state? Can I name a few activities?

I. Which activities will keep me in this state? Do I want to keep doing them?

J. How should I live my life moving forward given what has happened can't be changed?

K. When am I planning to get out of this situation?

L. Who will be impacted negatively if I don't improve?

M. Can I talk to someone close and express my inner feelings and become free from it?

N. Which new hobby will I cultivate and direct my energy in a positive direction?

O. What new activity will I initiate that resonates with me?

P. If I feel like crying, what is stopping me? Why not cry in loneliness or in the presence of a trusted person to vent my feelings and then alleviate my mood?

Q. What will be my next step to improve my situation?

R. By what day/time do I want to be happy again?

Step 3: Plan and act: As discussed in the previous chapter, depending on the way you would classify your emotions, the action plan can be prepared. The following is the summary.

- Low intensity for Short Time: Use awareness and understanding of situation (use above questionnaire).
- High Intensity for Short time: Quick Action tools are useful.

- High Intensity for Long Time: Quick Action and Deep Action tools are needed.
- Low Intensity for Long Time: Deep Action tools are needed.

Think about this: It is important to understand that life will have ups and downs. We all had some kind of setbacks, but whatever happened cannot be undone. We all have the right to feel sad if a dear one passes away or a relationship we cared about failed or we lost the job we enjoyed or any other major failure. Yes, we should be unhappy. Emotions are part of our life and they make us human. The point is we should not get stuck at one point. Life is precious. Life is a gift of nature. Eventually, we should move on and come out of the sad situation. We should pay tribute to what we cared about and then choose a positive way of living. Let us make the best of the life we have. Let us live a life of joy and satisfaction. It is what we deserve. Don't we?

15 Steps to implement

The following is one possible way to approach the situation. You may customize the following plan to optimize it for yourself.

(1) Which unwanted emotion/feeling/mood would you like to manage?

_____

(2) Classify your emotion on intensity-time spectrum.

_____

(3) What are the causes of this emotion?

_____

_____

_____

(4) Do you want to take control of the situation?

_____

(5) In how much time (days/month) do you want to have total control on the situation?

_____

_____

(6) Is there anything you can do (other than this action plan) to manage or control the situation? If yes, mention two things you may want to do to change the situation.

_____

_____

_____

(7) Mention two reasons for taking control of the situation.

_____

_____

(8) Have a look at the questionnaire in this chapter. Mention three questions that you think are most relevant to ask in your specific situation.

_____

_____

_____

_____

(9) Which of the "Quick Action" tools are you going to utilize? Mention your tools in detail. Mention three top priority tools.

_____

_____

_____

_____

(10) Which of the "Deep Action" tools will you utilize? Mention any two tools that you think are relevant for your situation.

_____

_____

_____

(11) Mention any two things that you believe you will be able to do easily. When will you begin?

_____

_____

_____

(12) Mention any two things you believe will be difficult to implement. Also mention how you will overcome the difficulty.

_____

_____

_____

(13) Do you have any specific mind-set, beliefs, social/personal/experiential conditionings that may prevent you from taking action? List them. How will you overcome them?

_____

_____

_____

(14) How will you be different and improved after you achieve your goal of having control over unwanted emotions? Can you specify two to five improvements in yourself?

_____

_____

_____

(15) What learning would you like to take with you
      for your improved future from this exercise or
      activities you have done here? Please summarize
      your learning.

      _____

      _____

      _____

Let us take right action to manage our mind. You may
customize any of the processes for your situation. You may
involve a mentor for the same.

CHAPTER 17

Fear

*If we can identify which of our fears are real
and which of them are fictitious, we are halfway
through the journey of curing the fictitious ones.*

What can cause fear? Let us imagine a few possible life situations that may make one fearful.

Alan was afraid of darkness since his childhood and one recent incident had intensified his fear. One day, he was walking down a street at night in the dark and he tripped over a sleeping dog. The dog suddenly woke up and started barking loudly. Alan was horrified to see such an angry dog and ran back home. Now, he has developed a phobia of darkness as a result of such an incident.

Jeff is afraid to face interviews. Whenever he goes for an interview, he remembers an incident from high school. One day, his English teacher asked him a question that he could not answer. The teacher rebuked him harshly in the presence of the entire class and Jeff was petrified. This memory was disturbing him. He had performed well academically in college, but he was still afraid to answer questions by authority figures. When interviewer starts asking questions, he loses confidence, gets nervous, becomes anxious, and cannot reply. He gets distressed even thinking about interview.

Maria is afraid of initiating new relationships. The last two times, she had horrible experiences. Her first boyfriend betrayed her. He promised to marry her but left her without even informing her. She later found out that he was dating another girl. Her second boyfriend tortured her a lot. In the beginning, the relationship was going smoothly. But as time passed, he started showing his true colors. For even trivial things, he would shout at her. He expected her to be perfect in every aspect. She could not tolerate the stressful relationship and eventually left him. Both the previous incidents have scared her. She is now afraid to begin a relationship. She becomes anxious thinking history may be repeated.

How does one handle fear?

Step 1: Acknowledge and accept: Fear comes in many forms and names. Here are a few words that describe this emotion with different intensity and context. Let us review them.

Fear	Fright	Scare	Intimidation	Distress
Panic	Horror	Terror	Shock	Phobia

So, if you are going through any of the above emotional states, let's first acknowledge and accept. This will open the door to change the situation.

Step 2: Examine and analyze:

Let us examine and analyze the following aspects.

- The root cause of the fear: This will throw light on understanding the situation.
- Intensity and time: We had discussed this in detail in previous chapters. Understanding this aspect will help us to use the right tools.

Note: Fear is not always bad. In many cases, fear is our response to a real danger. It is a survival mechanism for our body. Let us explore a few such situations.

- A person is afraid when she sees a car racing toward her. She stays away from the path of the car. In such cases, fear is an essential mechanism for survival.

- If you are in a jungle and you see a lion approaching you, fear is useful. When you see a snake approaching you, you may want to get away.
- If you see a building catching fire, you want to exit as early as possible. If the fear is triggered, it is fine.

So, the question is, "In which situations is the fear not useful? And when do we want to take control of it?" Well, many times, we extend life situations into "survival" type situations. Consider the following two examples.

1. Fear of rejection and failure: A person might be afraid to take risk or initiate any action, as he is afraid of rejection. One thing that might be happening in the person's mind is—he is taking rejection of a specific request as rejection of self. He thinks he is rejected as an individual when the other is just denying a specific request. Here, the fear arises due to overreaction and generalization. Such fear should be cured.

2. Phobias: People develop many types of phobias. Here, as in many occasions, they are amplifying a fear response up to the extent that the fear almost paralyzes them and they become very inefficient in doing something. Well, many times, there might be an understandable reason behind a phobia. For example, if any bad incident had happened in someone's youth when he was walking alone in the darkness, he might develop a phobia of darkness. And we may understand his reason. He has a valid point. Now, the question is, should he live with

this phobia or does he want to cure it? I would choose the cure.

What are different types of fear? What causes fear? The following are some of the thoughts.

- Fear of failure, fear of exams, fear of competition
- Fear of rejection, fear of taking initiative
- Fear of death and ill health
- Fear of losing a relationship even when the relationship is horrible
- Fear of social defamation if any secret is revealed
- Fear of "what society will think"
- Fear of losing money if investment is risky
- Fear of public speaking
- Fear of learning new things, doing something for the first time
- Fear of any specific aspect of life due to past experiences (example: fear of darkness)
- Fear of approaching an authority or interacting with someone who is harsh or unpredictable
- Inferiority complex due to anything
- Phobias

Step 3: Plan and act: As discussed in previous chapters, depending on the way you would classify your emotion, the action plan can be prepared. The following is the summary.

- Low Intensity for Short Time: Use awareness and understanding of situation (use questionnaire given in chapter 16: Questions A to R).
- High Intensity for Short time: Quick Action tools are useful.

- High Intensity for Long Time: Quick Action and Deep Action tools are needed.
- Low Intensity for Long Time: Deep Action tools are needed.

Note: Please see the "15 steps to implement" given at the end of the chapter on "sadness." It might be helpful with appropriate customization for this emotion.

A few additional thoughts on specific fears are as follows.

- Fear of failure and rejection: Don't assume that you need to be perfect. Accept the reality that all individuals fail at some point in some way. There is no need to have a perfect expectation from the self. Thomas Edison failed hundreds of times while he was inventing the light bulb. He was optimistic; he continued to approach the problem in new ways and eventually became successful.

- Inferiority complexes: We are not perfect. Everyone has strengths as well as weaknesses. If I have a specific weakness, I may focus on taking right actions that will improve me in that aspect. I need to be ready to learn and improve.

Challenge yourself: I will not let fear control my life and future.

CHAPTER 18

Anger

*Anger may or may not hurt or harm the person
against whom it is targeted. It definitely harms
the person who goes through it.*

What makes us angry? Let us imagine a few possible life situations that can make one angry.

"You always leave your clothes lying all over the place," shouted Jill with anger.

"Look, I had a busy day at work and I am tired. Don't you always taunt me like this," Jack shouted back.

"You never listen to me. Maybe you don't care for me anymore," complained Jill in an irritated tone.

Now, Jack's volume was increasing, "I care for you, but it does not mean I do everything you say. Leave me alone. I want to relax." Jack was now agitated. He sat down relaxed on the couch in the drawing room and turned on the television.

"You never pay attention to me." Jill was now fuming with anger. She walked into the bedroom, slamming the door.

"Have you ever completed your work properly? Look at these sales data. I want to see them going up!" Bob's manager shouted at him with anger. The manager continued, "Any new college hire will perform better than you. You are not serious about your job."

Bob was now fuming with anger. His face was turning red. "The way management wants to see increase in sales is not realistic in this economy," Bob argued back. "We are working as hard as we can, but we are not magicians," he ferociously argued.

"I don't want to listen to such excuses. Go out and come back only after you have better sales data," the manager ordered, fuming with anger. Bob spent the rest of his day being upset.

How does one handle "anger?"

Step 1: Acknowledge and accept: Anger comes in many forms. Here are a few words that describe this emotion.

Angry	Upset	Agitated	Annoyed	Irritated
Ferocious	Raging	Fuming	Wrathful	Provoked

So, if you are going through any of the above emotional states, let's first acknowledge and accept it. This will open the door to change the situation.

Step 2: Examine and analyze:

Let us examine and analyze the following aspects.

- The root cause of the emotion: This will throw light on understanding the situation.
- Intensity and time: We have discussed this in detail in the previous chapters. Understanding this aspect will help us use the right tools.

Let us begin our analysis. What can cause anger? The following are a few possible reasons. The purpose is to think and put forward your reason or reasons for anger. Once we identify the reason, we may do further analysis.

Some possible causes of anger:

- Day-to-day turbulences in personal and professional life
- Incidents during traffic jams and daily traveling

- Minor or major insults by someone at the workplace or from family
- Minor or major injustices (including not getting what we deserve)
- Unexpected and inappropriate behavior/reaction from others
- Betrayal in relationships
- Incidents of being cheated or hurt, especially by a trusted one
- Tension in family relationships

What makes you angry? Please list the causes in the blank lines below.

- _____
- _____
- _____

Step 3: Plan and act: As discussed in previous chapters, depending on the way you would classify your emotion, the action plan can be prepared. The following is the summary.

- Low Intensity for Short Time: Use awareness and understanding of situation (use questionnaire given in chapter 16: Questions A to R).
- High Intensity for Short time: Quick Action tools are useful.
- High Intensity for Long Time: Quick Action and Deep Action tools are needed.
- Low Intensity for Long Time: Deep Action tools are needed.

Note: Please see the "15 steps to implement" given at the end of the chapter on "sadness." It might be helpful with appropriate customization for this emotion.

Where and when is "anger" useful?

Sometimes, anger can be used as a tool if all other tools failed to convey the right message to someone. The message can be to follow discipline or not to get involved in improper behavior. It is reasonable to become angry for the right reason at the right person.

Challenge yourself: I will not let anyone push the buttons and make me angry.

In that moment of rage and anger,
I happened to see myself in the mirror.
My skin was red, eyes tensed and wide open,
Face was ugly and bad; that I don't want to see often.

Blood pressure mounted, heartbeat was raised,
It appeared to me that my body was punished.
For what reason am I going through this anguish?
I realized I was hurting myself for someone else's deeds.

Because they were dishonest and she misbehaved,
He broke a promise for which I punished myself.
I will not become angry. I am resolved.
Why suffer for someone else's fault?

CHAPTER 19

Guilt and Shame

*We can prevent ourselves from guilt and
shame if we choose and take the right action
at the right time in the right way.*

What can cause guilt and shame? Let us imagine a
possible life situation.

Tom and Jeff were competitors since their early
school days. When they joined the same college, their
competition intensified. Just a week before their final
exams, Tom stole all the lecture notes and books from
Jeff's room; that eventually left Jeff unprepared and beaten
in the exam results. Thought Tom beat him in the exams,
gradually he started developing a sense of guilt for what
he had done to Jeff. He was ashamed and regretful for his
act of theft. When he learned that Jeff lost his scholarship
as a result of his insufficient exam score, Tom was in deep

remorse, as he never intended such consequences for Jeff. He regretted his action. He was ashamed for what he did to Jeff.

How does one handle guilt and shame?

Step 1: Acknowledge and accept: Here are a few words that describe this emotion.

Shame   Guilt   Remorse   Regret   Repentance
Sorry   Embarrassed Humiliated Apologetic Dishonored

So, if you are going through any of the above emotional states, let's first acknowledge and accept it. This will open the door to change the situation.

Step 2: Examine and analyze:

Let us examine and analyze the following aspects.

- Root causes of guilt and shame: Finding what has caused the guilt and shame may throw some light on what we may do to come out of the situation.
- Intensity and time: We have discussed this in detail in previous chapters. Understanding this aspect will help us use the right tools.

What can cause shame and guilt?

- Performing below par in a critical situation. Eg.—a game, competition, exam, family situation, etc.
- Acting against normal structure of society and culture
- Doing something evil and realizing it later
- Hurting someone innocent by mistake
- Taking revenge and then realizing it was not needed and realizing revenge was an act of false pride
- Not taking timely action for a situation, the situation then aggravates and ends up in disaster.
- Many more causes and situations that you may like to add here.

Some questions to be asked:

- What should I do in future so that I don't end up feeling shame and guilt?
- What should I *not* do in future so that I don't end up feeling shame and guilt?
- Which action should I take to reduce the feeling of shame and guilt?
- What steps can I take to improve my image in my own eye, in my family's eyes, and in society?
- Are my heart and mind free from evil intentions?
- Did I apologize to the person I have hurt?
- What can I do for the person who unnecessarily suffered because of me?

Step 3: Plan and act: As discussed in previous chapters, depending on the way you would classify your emotion, the action plan can be prepared. The following is the summary.

- Low Intensity for Short Time: Use awareness and understanding of situation (use questionnaire given in chapter 16: Questions A to R).
- High Intensity for Short time: Quick Action tools are useful.
- High Intensity for Long Time: Quick Action and Deep Action tools are needed.
- Low Intensity for Long Time: Deep Action tools are needed.

Note: Please see the "15 steps to implement" given at the end of the chapter on "sadness." It might be helpful with appropriate customization for this emotion.

Challenge yourself: I will do my best not to end up in the situation that makes me embarrassed. I will apologize to the right person at the right time if needed.

CHAPTER 20

Hate, Envy, and Vengeance

"He who seeks vengeance must dig two graves:
one for his enemy and the other for himself."
—Chinese Proverb

What makes us feel hatred, envy, and full of vengeance? Let us imagine a few possible life situations.

Hate: Mona hates people who don't keep their house clean. When her cousin visited her for two weeks, it was a nightmare for her. Her cousin was never careful in cleaning her room. Mona politely suggested that she keep things clean, but she did not understand. This developed a kind of detestation in Mona for her cousin. When her cousin left, Mona had to clean her entire house, and she felt disgusted to see how the guest room was. She now loathes anyone who does not keep one's house clean and does not permit such individuals to stay in her house.

Envy: Mark was jealous of all the praise Mike received from their boss. Both of them worked hard, but somehow, Mike was able to highlight his work at the right time in the right way that made him more noticeable. In the annual review, when Mike was promoted to the manager's position, Mark was envious of his success. That was the position Mark coveted, and now it went to Mike just because of some circumstantial situations in which Mike was able to highlight his work more effectively.

Vengeance: When Jeff came to know what Tom has done to him, he was full of vengeance for Tom. He was deeply hurt. He started to plan to retaliate. He wanted to take revenge, but when Tom apologized and promised to pay the money he had lost with the scholarship, Jeff's desire for retaliation was quenched.

How to handle the difficult feelings of hatred, envy, and vengeance?

Step 1: Acknowledge and accept: Here are a few words that describe these emotions.

Hate	dislike	disgust	antipathy	abhorrence
Envy	jealousy	covetousness	craving	spite
Vengeance	resentment	revenge	antagonism	retribution

So, if you are going through any of the above emotional states, let's first acknowledge and accept it. This will open the door to change the situation.

Step 2: Examine and analyze:

Let us examine and analyze the following aspects.

- Root causes of hatred, envy, and vengeance: Finding what has caused the emotion may throw some light on what we may do to come out of the situation.
- Intensity and time: We have discussed this in detail in previous chapters. Understanding this aspect will help us to use the right tools.

What can cause hatred?

- Something or someone we do not like for any reason
- Someone who always creates obstacles and troubles for us
- Someone who is not decent, polite, or well mannered.
- Something or someone who somehow puts us in a negative state of mind
- Many more reasons you may note down.

What can cause envy?

- Someone's achievement that we believe we also deserve
- Someone's achievement that we may not be able to achieve
- Someone wins or achieves what he does not deserve

- Someone performs better than we did to win or achieve something
- Someone's achievement that we may think he has achieved by improper means

What can cause vengeance?

- Someone who betrayed us
- Someone harmed us and did injustice when we were weak
- Someone robbed something from us
- Someone insulted us or humiliated us at the wrong time and wrong place for the wrong reason
- Someone sacrificed us for his achievements
- Many more reasons that you may like to include here.

Some questions to ponder upon:

- What is the purpose of my life? Do I want to waste my life in the pursuit of vengeance?
- If I am envious of someone, how can I achieve qualities needed to achieve what he has achieved?
- Why should I hate someone because he does not fit in to my way of living?
- If someone insults me, why should I react? How about reacting by performing better?
- How should I divert my negative energy into creative work? What creative thing should I do?

Step 3: Plan and act: As discussed in previous chapters, depending on the way you would classify your emotion, the action plan can be prepared. The following is the summary.

- Low intensity for Short Time: Use awareness and understanding of situation (use questionnaire given in Chapter 16: Questions A to R)
- High Intensity for Short time: Quick Action tools are useful
- High Intensity for Long Time: Quick Action and Deep Action tools are needed
- Low Intensity for Long Time: Deep Action tools are needed.

Note: Please see the "15 steps to implement" given at the end of chapter on "sadness." It might be helpful with appropriate customization for this emotion.

Challenge yourself: The world may not be always fair to us. I acknowledge this. I may use all fair legal systems if I seek justice. At the same time, I need to live the life I want to live. Divert the negative energy to creative work. I may express my emotions to the people I trust.

CHAPTER 21

Happiness

Happiness is the lubricant for the machine
of life when it passes through adversities.

In most of the situations, happiness is a desirable emotion. Who on earth does not want to be happy?

What makes us happy? Imagine one possible scenario. When I met my sister after she returned from a tour, I was *glad* to see her. My parents and I missed her *jovial* nature that used to make our family time memorable. She surprised Mom by giving her a pink woolen sweater. Mom was very *joyful* to receive it. I was *delighted* to receive my favorite chocolate as my gift. After dinner, we sat down to hear her stories. She was very *excited* to describe all the interesting places she had been to. Many times, I could see a sense of *ecstasy* on her face. We talked till late in the night. For my dad, to see his family having such a wonderful time was a *blissful* event.

How does one elicit happiness?

The question for the emotion of happiness is upside down compared to undesired emotions like sadness or anger. Here, we want to have happiness as and when we desire it. So, our approach will be upside down as well.

Step 1: Acknowledge and accept: Happiness comes to our life in various flavors. Our language has several words to describe it. Let us examine a few such words.

Happy	glad	cheerful	jovial	pleased
Ebullient	ecstatic	euphoric	blissful	thrilled

Let us acknowledge that there is a need of this emotion during any specific occasion or in life in general. Someone might have a pessimistic nature, a depressed mood for any reason, and he may want to be happy. Here is the opportunity to elicit happiness. Once we accept the need, we may work forward.

Step 2: Examine and analyze:

For eliciting a positive emotion, the process of examination and analysis will be different compared to negative and unwanted emotions. Here, the goal will be to find out what can make someone happy.

- What may elicit happiness: We need to think and brainstorm about what can make you happy. Examining all the "Quick Action Tools" can be a starting point.

- Intensity and time: Here, the goal will be to start from low intensity short time situations and expand it to any of the required intensity-time spectrum.

Questions to ask:

- Which memory can trigger happiness now?
- Which sensory inputs can make me happy?
- How should I plan to relive the moments that can make me happy? Should I use photos, movies, any special thing (e.g., special purchase from vacation, birthday card, etc.) to trigger the memory?
- Examine all the aspects of Quick Action tools and find out what can be instrumental for this purpose.

Step 3: Plan and act: Once our goal is clear, we may plan as per the classification of intensity and time.

- Low Intensity for Short Time: Use awareness and understanding of the need for happiness.
- High Intensity for Short time: Quick Action tools are useful.
- High Intensity for Long Time: Quick Action and Deep Action tools are needed.
- Low Intensity for Long Time: Deep Action tools are needed.

On which occasions, do we not want to be happy? The following are a few possible scenarios.

- I am overjoyed, ebullient, excited. Now, at the end of the day, I want to sleep properly. This emotion may not let me sleep. It may keep me up. And I know my body wants to rest.

o Solution: Use any progressive relaxation technique or meditate for some time.

- I am ebullient and my emotions are hindering me from focusing on my work—it can be any work. Now, I want to focus.

  o Solution: Use any progressive relaxation technique or meditate for some time.

- I am excited and I need to go to a social or professional function where seriousness is needed. Imagine this situation. I am thrilled with joy due to some reason, and I attend a meeting where my manager declares that sales are below expectations and next quarter seems difficult. Here, I need to come to the "here and now," get involved in the situation seriously, leaving behind my personal reason of ecstasy.

- Once in a while, we may feel happy about another's damage or loss. There might be someone whom we dislike and envy. And he may end up in an unfavorable situation. One voice inside us may say, "This is what he deserves." The other voice may say, "Well, I may not like him, but I wish only good for everyone."

- Feel free to add more such situations here. Life is very interesting and dynamic.

Challenge yourself: Make sure you remain cheerful. When you meet another person, greet him or her with a cheerful voice. Smile. Do small things to make others happy in your family and with your friends. Make sure to greet everyone on birthdays, anniversaries, on graduation, on any special achievements, and become the beacon of happiness. Learn to look at the positive side of everything. Life is precious.

CHAPTER 22

Love

An unconditional love is a rare phenomenon.

In many situations, love is a desired emotion. We all want to love and be loved. Love can be between a child and parents, siblings, spouses, friends, mentor and mentee, and so on. Love also has an undesirable aspect if it turns into infatuation, lust, obsession, or mania.

Please note that love is such a huge topic that volumes have been written on it. Here, our discussion will be focused on specific situations. We will explore two situations.

(1) The first situation is how can we elicit the consistency of love as a positive emotion when needed. Once in a while, we may go through a rough patch in our close personal relationships when love seems to be drying out. This may happen in any relationship. But deep inside, we

know and trust the person. Deep inside, we know this is just turbulence in a lifelong relationship. Once we realize this, we may want to take a positive turn and get back to a full expression of love. Can there be any other such situation or reason? Yes. We may have our own reasons and situations where we need to express and enhance the love we have in our heart. Please feel free to list them.

(2) The second situation is how can we manage this strong emotion if it turns into an obsession or mania. The obsession or mania may be for an individual, for any specific thing, for any specific achievement, or any other thing. Consider the first case of obsession for an individual. Many times, we may end up in one-sided affection. If someone does not like us, it is his or her choice. We should respect the feelings and move forward positively. Well, it is easier said than done. It is very difficult. And this is the reason we want to handle this situation carefully with the tools we have developed.

We will explore both the situations separately. We will have a different set of questions to explore for both of them. So, let us first explore the positive side of "love."

1: How does one elicit love or consistency of love when required?

Step 1: Acknowledge and accept: The following are a few words that represent the positive side of love in our language.

Love   affection   attachment admiration   respect
Liking appreciation friendship companionship worship

Let us accept and acknowledge the need to work on this emotion.

Step 2: Examine and analyze:

For eliciting a positive emotion, the process of examination and analysis will be different compared to negative and unwanted emotions. We will take the following two aspects of the analysis.

- What may elicit love? We need to find out what can maintain your love or make you more loveable. The "Quick Action Tools" can be a starting point for the brainstorming.
- Intensity and time: Here, the goal will be to start from "low intensity short time" situation and expand it to any of the required intensity-time spectrum.

Questions to ask and points to ponder about:

- Life is full of ups and downs. What creates ebb and flow in my love for the people I care for?
- I know everyone is selfish at some level. I should appreciate what he/she has done for me so far.

- Everyone's focus wanders once in a while. Let's get back to the mainstream of life.
- Everyone makes mistakes sometimes. No one is perfect. Let me forgive him/her.
- He/she may not express love for me as I expect. His/her way of expression might be different. Deep down in his/her heart, he/she cares for me.
- In a tough economy, he/she is focusing on earning for our family. Family may not appear to be the point of focus now, but he/she is doing everything for us alone. Let me support him/her.
- Can I focus on the big picture of life and forgive a few acts of the person I love.
- How can I communicate my dissatisfaction to him/her so that he/she understands?
- What should I do so that he/she is happy with this relationship?
- What exactly does he/she expect from me?
- Let us talk in detail, vent out all frustration, and be clear about our future.
- How is this relationship important for me? How can I stabilize it?
- Till today, what sacrifices has he/she made for me? Should I not appreciate them?
- What specific aspects of my behavior hurt him/her?
- Is it not his/her right to express dissatisfaction in the relationship? This is the first step to strengthen it.
- I might have behaved in a similar way if I were going through such a difficult time.
- His/her behavior might not be intentional.

There are many more points to ponder and questions to be asked. I hope this will give you a starting point for thinking. Please think and add more points here.

Step 3: Plan and act: Once our goal is clear, we may plan as per the classification of intensity and time.

- Low Intensity for Short Time: Use awareness and understanding of situation (use questionnaire given in chapter 16: Questions A to R with appropriate modifications).
- High Intensity for Short time: Quick Action tools are useful.
- High Intensity for Long Time: Quick Action and Deep Action tools are needed.
- Low Intensity for Long Time: Deep Action tools are needed.

Note: Please see the "15 steps to implement" given at the end of the chapter on "sadness." Modify them when needed. It might be helpful with appropriate customization for this emotion.

Challenge yourself:

Many relationships have ups and downs. In such situations, we may extend forgiveness and flexibility. We may find out what can strengthen the relationship. And we may extend the unconditional love to the people we really care about. Mother Teresa once said, "I have found the paradox, that if you love until it hurts, there can be no more hurt, only more love."

2: How does one manage this strong emotion if it turns into obsession or mania?

Step 1: Acknowledge and accept: The following are a few words that represent the side of love that we may want to get control over.

Infatuation	lust	obsession	passion	mania
Lunacy	craze	adulation	compulsion	covetousness

Lets us accept and acknowledge the need to work on this emotion.

Step 2: Examine and analyze:

For managing unwanted emotions, we may take the same approach that we took for managing sadness and anger. Let us begin with the following two analyses.

- Root cause of emotion: Understanding the root cause of the emotion and analyzing the situation in a broader perspective of life will throw light on understanding and examining the situation. This can be achieved by asking ourselves questions and by pondering important points.
- Intensity and time: We have discussed this in detail in the previous chapters. Understanding this aspect will help us use the right tools.

Questions to ask and points to ponder about:

- How many people have you met or seen who are unhappy after achieving what they once coveted?

There are many couples who end up in divorce. Once, they meant the world to each other. And hardly any couple will begin their life wishing for separation, but as time passes, they realize they are not meant for each other. Now, the question for me is, how do I know my relation with the person I am obsessed with will never end up in such realization?

- There are many people who achieved their goals, but after achieving it, they felt emptiness inside. They are not happy with what they have achieved and look for something else. Am I sure I am seeking happiness at the right place? How do I know that the desire is not driven by ego? I might have failed to achieve this and my ego is hurt. So I am obsessed to have it, but if I analyze things, I may realize that there are many other things that can make me happy!

- How do I know I am chasing my ego, that I just want to win? Once I achieve what I want, the achievement may not matter to me.

- There are many more people who love me and care for me. I need to care for them and live a decent life. I want to make sure I don't do anything silly.

- In the big picture of my identity and life, how much does this matter?

- How can one person or one thing paralyze my mind?

- If you feel the need to cry or express your frustration, do it where you are comfortable. Find a place which is safe for you in terms of expressing your sad emotions. After being unhappy for some time and venting out your emotions, come out positively.

- Talk to the family or friend and vent out your feelings. Discussion with a trusted one will alleviate the burden.
- Go out in the world and notice that good people are all around. They all are unique. Many of them are worth your love and affection.
- Why squander a life for someone who does not care for you?
- Life is big. Small things keep happening.
- Which new hobby will I cultivate and how will I direct my energy in a positive direction?
- What new activity will I initiate that resonates with me?
- Which one step can I take that will make me smile? Maybe, let me look at the mirror and make faces. Or I will smile in the mirror.
- Make sure you read and contemplate on the chapters of the "concept of self" and "purpose of life."

Step 3: Plan and act: Once our goal is clear, we may plan as per the classification of intensity and time.

- Low Intensity for Short Time: Use awareness and understanding of situation (use questionnaire given in chapter 16: Questions A to R with appropriate modifications).
- High Intensity for Short time: Quick Action tools are useful.
- High Intensity for Long Time: Quick Action and Deep Action tools are needed.
- Low Intensity for Long Time: Deep Action tools are needed.

Note: Please see the "15 steps to implement" given at the end of the chapter on "sadness." Modify them when needed. It might be helpful with appropriate customization for this emotion.

Challenge yourself:

When I was little, I used to cry for chocolates and toys. If I didn't get chocolate or if my toy was broken, I used to cry like the world was ending. If I look back and analyze it, how important are they in today's perspective? They were important for me, but not important enough to feel like the end of the world. However, in that moment, they really meant the world to me.

In a similar way, there is someone or something for which I am overemotional today, but in the big picture of life, it is possible that if I looked back twenty years from now, this specific person or thing may look like the obsession for those chocolates and toys. It does not mean the person or thing is not important. They are important. The point is not getting them is not the end of the world.

PART V

MANAGING FEELINGS AND MOODS

CHAPTER 23

Selected Undesired Feelings and Moods

We better manage our feelings and moods
before they start managing us.

In this chapter, we will dive deeper into managing unwanted feelings and moods. Our approach will be similar to that of the negative emotions. In addition, we will explore selected feelings and moods individually. The following is the summary of the steps.

Step 1: Acknowledge and accept: The first step is to acknowledge that we are going through an undesired state of mind. Many times, our feelings and moods are genuine. A person is deeply hurt, as his loved one betrayed him. Someone may get frustrated as things are out of his control. The situation might be genuine. The next step would be to accept that we need to change it.

Step 2: Examine and analyze: In this chapter, we will ponder about selected feelings and moods in detail. Let us have a closer look at them. Let us think from a different viewpoint. This thought process may give rise to better understanding and direct us toward positive end results. This understanding may strengthen our desire to come out of an unwanted state of mind. We will explore selected feelings and moods one at a time. You may analyze the feelings and moods with reference to intensity and time as discussed in the previous chapters.

Step 3: Plan and act: As discussed in previous chapters, depending on the way you would classify your feelings and moods, actions can be planned. The following is the summary.

- Low Intensity for Short Time: Use awareness and understanding of the situation (use questionnaire given in chapter 16: Questions A to R; see the discussion on selected feelings and moods in this chapter).
- High Intensity for Short time: Quick Action tools are useful.
- High Intensity for Long Time: Quick Action and Deep Action tools are needed.
- Low Intensity for Long Time: Deep Action tools are needed.

Note: Please see the "15 steps to implement" given at the end of the chapter on "sadness." It might be helpful with appropriate customization for feelings and moods under consideration.

Now, let us explore selected feelings and moods in some detail.

Lethargy

Time is ticking. All of us have finite and limited time. One day, without one's permission, the heart may stop. Many times, the death will not even give us a warning to wind up the life properly. Other times, it may give some indications when it will end. One might be diagnosed with terminal cancer and the end would be imminent. In some way, life will end. No one lives forever.

Every second is precious. Every minute, hour, and day is precious. A minute wasted is a minute not lived. A day wasted is a day not lived. At the end, if we look back to analyze and calculate how many days we have lived and how many days we have *not* lived, we want to be on the positive side of the equation.

Lethargy is the best way to waste this precious life. If one wants to become an expert on squandering the opportunity that life and time give, then being lethargic is the best option. But remember, there is no second chance when it comes to time. Time will march forward whether you use it or lose it.

Why not live fully each and every moment of your life? Why not be active and action-oriented? Why not procrastinate procrastination itself? If determined, what can stop you from taking a step toward your desired goal? And these small steps eventually transform into a journey and a voyage. Life is calling you. It is waiting for you. You can choose to remain inactive; you can choose to become active. For every choice, there will be some consequences. Every action taken leads toward a goal. Every action missed keeps you away from the goal. So what are you waiting for? Come on and live your life so vivaciously that if Time had the opportunity to live a human life, it would choose yours.

Disappointment

> "Blessed is he who expects nothing, for he shall never be disappointed"
>
> —Alexander Pope.

Disappointment is a companion of desires and expectations. If we choose desires and expectations, we have already chosen disappointment. Why? Well, every desire and expectation will not be fulfilled.

Ok. Now we know, we need to get ready for the disappointment. So, how does one face it? How does one come out winning? One approach would be to look at disappointment as an indicator of change. Either we need to change the way to the goal or the goal itself.

I remember what Thomas Edison said when he failed thousands of times while inventing the light bulb. He said, "I have not failed. I have just found ten thousand ways that won't work." Here, Edison is considering "failure" as an indicator to change the way to a goal. If my goal is to become financially independent and if one of my investments fails, I may feel disappointed. Here, I need to change the way to my goal. I don't want to get stuck in the feeling of disappointment. I need to start looking for alternate ways of investment.

The other option is to realize one needs to change the goal. Suppose I want to become a singer and I fail in several attempts. This may indicate that singing might not be my forte. I may try acting, painting, writing, sports, or any other talent. It is OK to quit. I need not keep attempting success and waste my time if I realize what I am doing is not my strength.

If I am disappointed by my annual appraisal, it is time to change either my performance at the job or the job itself. If my manager wants me to do my job in a different way, I change the performance. If I realize this manager will never appreciate me, then it is time to change the job.

Hurt

When a trusted one disappoints us, it hurts. The feeling of hurt might be genuine. Once hurt, what does one do? How does one move ahead? Consider the following quote.

> "No one deserves your tears. Those who deserve it will never make you cry."
> —Gabriel García Márquez

Let us redefine "trusted one" with above new light. In a short time span, when things are normal, many people will behave well with us. But when tough times come, people show their true colors. We discover and realize that people we trusted are not worth trusting. It might be a difficult fact to accept, but the sooner we accept, the earlier we are relieved from the pain of hurt.

Well, you may say we should give the benefit of the doubt to the trusted one. There might be some kind of misunderstanding. There might be ineffective communication. There might be differences in beliefs that might have led to extended altercations. How does one deal with such situations?

Here, we may expand our flexibility. We may become open to unexpected reactions and behaviors. We may say yes to uncertainty. We may accept that we might not always be able to anticipate the behavior of a loved one. We may let ourselves be more vulnerable.

Can we become very strong, very quickly adaptable, be a quick learner, and malleable so that when the unexpected happens, we expand the boundary of our "expected" behavior and adjust? Everyone is selfish in some way. This selfishness may end up hurting us.

Can we love unconditionally? Can we expect nothing in exchange for our love for someone? Well, this seems a superhuman quality, but it might be possible to have it for at least selected individuals during critical times.

Loneliness

Many times, this feeling is uncomfortable and a person seeks the company of others. He may divert his attention to reading, watching television, or surfing the Internet or engage in any other activity so that he forgets he is alone.

In a much deeper sense, all of us are alone. We are born alone. We will die alone. Someone may argue that there were many people around us at the time of birth or will be there near the deathbed. Understand that the event of birth and death happens to an individual only. Whoever is around there does not impact the experience of birth or death in any deeper sense. For these processes, a person is alone.

In everyday life, we sleep alone. Well, there might be someone accompanying us, but the event of sleep happens to an individual only. Now, you may guess I will expand this loneliness to many more activities. We breathe and absorb oxygen alone. We eat and digest alone. We watch a game and we enjoy it alone. You may say, "I go to watch games in a group." Well, a group has some influence, but the experience is yours alone. If you are sick while watching a game, you experience it differently. If you are worried about some important issue, your experience is different.

One possible way to look at life is that we might have many people around, but in the core experience, we are alone. Accept this fact and become comfortable with the self. If you are comfortable with yourself, you will not feel loneliness. Refer to the chapters on the concept of self and purpose of life. Think. Ponder. Understand life. You may develop a joy of just being alive. Life is a miracle. You don't need anyone else to be with you to enjoy it.

Not comfortable with the above idea? Well, there is a way for you as well. Identify the ways to get involved in activities you like, participate in charity and social activities, help others, explore social media, and you may no longer experience loneliness.

Worthlessness

When you came to the world, you made your parents smile. They were thrilled to have you. While growing up, you made your friends smile. However small, you contributed in making them happy. As an adult, you contributed to the family, society, and country. If you have bought anything, you have contributed to the growth of the economy. If you have voted a single time, you have contributed to strengthen democracy. Small drops of water builds an ocean. If every drop thinks that it is not significant and does not remain in the ocean, the ocean will dry up. Every drop of water counts.

Many times, people may not tell you how precious you are, as they might be busy. Whether anyone tells you or not, you are precious. You are precious for yourself, family, and friends.

Don't let others define your worthiness. You are the consciousness who can comprehend and appreciate this universe. A stone can't wonder at the majestic ocean. A lion, called the king of the jungle, can't dance to melodious songs and enjoy the music. The most intelligent bird can't understand language and appreciate a poem. You can. You are unique. You are special.

Look into world history. Many extraordinary achievers had begun their lives very ordinarily. Thomas Edison and

Steve Jobs are examples. Yes, you can also contribute to mankind if you really have the desire. People may or may not appreciate you always, but it does not take away all the things you have done for many lives.

If you are disabled or you think you don't have any specific skill, think again. Helen Keller lost her ability to see and hear in childhood but became an eminent personality, who made a difference in many lives. If you believe in yourself, if you have courage to do what you want, you can also achieve many heights.

So, forget if others appreciate you or not. Focus on how you can make a difference.

Boredom

We want novelty. We want change. How about taking a small vacation? How about spending a weekend doing something new? These activities will give us some relief. And, in addition, they can bring in novelty to our otherwise mundane routines. Let us see if there is any scope for this.

How about trying out a different lunch or dinner at a different restaurant? How about different coffee or tea? How about taking a new route to work? I may like thriller movies. How about watching a comedy or drama for a change?

There are lots of opportunities where we can bring in novelty. It might be as silly as changing the mouth freshener or toothpaste, changing the soap or bathing liquid, wearing different perfume, changing breakfast, trying out new fashionable clothes, changing something in daily traveling, going to a different grocery store, choosing a different garden or road for daily walking, watching a new channel on TV, exploring the Internet, contacting a friend of school days and knowing how is he doing, spending a weekend for social service or helping the needy, and so many other things. Let us explore a few more creative ideas and find out how small changes in life can bring in novelty.

Here is one more possible approach. Change the way you see the situation. If you are watching a movie, think from a protagonist's viewpoint: how he can do better. Think how an antagonist, music director, director, producer, audience, critic, and others will view this movie. If you are stuck in a boring job, see how an unemployed person will look at this situation if he had this job. Look from the perspective of a person who, due to a family situation, could not afford the education needed to have your job. Look as if a person in an underdeveloped place in the world will feel if he is at your place. Thinking differently may reveal that it might not be that boring!

Nervousness

How would an astronaut, stepping on the moon, have managed his nervousness? How would a pilot manage his mind facing a severe weather disturbance up in the sky? It would be a matter of life and death.

Whether it is a job interview, meeting an important person for the first time, appearing in an exam for the first or second time, doing something new for the first time, trying to attempt something one more time after previous failure, playing or watching a critical moment in a sports match, awaiting a result of something we care about, we may feel nervous. Why? What causes nervousness and how does one handle it?

We may feel nervous because of uncertainty. The moment that will unfold may go toward our desired or undesired outcome. Even if it is not a life-and-death situation, in our failure, we may feel like we are missing something significant. If we embrace uncertainty, nervousness will start fading away.

The need of the moment is calmness, focus, self-belief, using all our abilities to achieve the desired outcome, and the ability to face an undesired result if things go wrong.

One approach to manage nervousness is to be in the "here and now." We need to develop the ability to remain at a place, sense the situation, remain in the present, and act. Our focus should be on what our eyes see, what our ears hear. Notice the details of the place, what is the construction, furniture, surroundings, luminosity, freshness, people around us, if there is any fragrance in the air, and various sounds. It can be any place of challenge—a playground, an operation theatre, an interview room, a place where crucial discussions will happen, and so on. And, of course, we need to remain in the present, leaving behind limiting memories and undesirable imaginations. Being in the "here and now" gives us serenity. We need to focus and access our inner strength. We need to do our best and leave the rest for the future.

Frustration

Take a deep breath and relax. We are not always in control of the situation. If we can't change the situation, change the way we look at the situation. Let us not fight against it. Let us accept it, wish things will improve soon, and focus on what we can do now. In frustration, we are not at our best, and steps we take might not be optimal in the given situation. We may end up performing below our capability. If we calm down and relax, we will soon be able to handle the situation more efficiently.

Relax and flow in the present when frustrated with life's circumstances and situations. You may plan an alternate activity that you may do to utilize your time, like thinking on any important project, calling a friend, working on personal mobile devices, reading, listening to music to relax, or any other activity you may like.

Many times, frustration is due to mismatch of expectation. Many times, our expectations are close to perfection. The flight must always be on time. The traffic must be less. If I try ten times, I must succeed at least once. Life may not be perfect and we need to get ready to accept it.

Many times, we may expect behavior from others with an incomplete understanding of others' situations. This may give rise to frustration. Communicating the expectation may solve the problem. We may try to change others' habits and end up frustrated. Conversely, we may get frustrated if another person tries to change us. One possible option would be not to get involved in changing someone or something unless the situation is critical.

In all cases, observe the frustration. Flow with your life. Observe what happens to the mind and body in frustration. Observe the breathing pattern. Just remain witness to the state of mind. Focus on good things you can do at this moment. Gradually, you will get proper control over the situation.

Anxiety

What is anxiety? We have the ability to imagine and to recall memory. We can end up recalling a terrible incident or we may imagine a horrible situation in the future. Once we have such thoughts in our mind, it may trigger a panic response. This panic response can paralyze our rational thought process to some degree, and we may end up worried and with negative emotions. Such a restless state of mind is a big aspect of what we may refer to as anxiety. Anxiety may impact the body as well.

The first aspect to determine is the cause of anxiety. Once we understand the cause, we may take the appropriate action.

Is the anxiety caused by something in reality? If things are not based in reality, we need to calm down, using any of the techniques we discussed. If we are warring due to something imagined, we need to get in touch with reality.

Observe the imagination. Observe how this imagination is impacting our mind.

If it is based on something real, we need to take action to avoid any undesired situation in life. We need to focus on what things we can do to prevent what we don't want. We may discuss it with our close friends or mentors. This will help us vent our tension as well as give us feedback on the plan of action.

If we are responding to a situation with exaggeration, we need to check our imagination. Things may go wrong beyond our imagination. But until the worst happens, let us not project it. And we better spend time planning to prevent the worst from happening rather than worrying about it.

If we are anxious due to an event in the past, we first need to understand that we can't change the past. We need to revive any good memory from the past and focus on it. We may use any of the Quick Action tools to reduce the intensity of anxiety. Then we may use Deep Action tools to look at the bigger perspective of life.

CHAPTER 24

Selected Desired Feelings and Moods

*The way to elicit desired feelings and
moods encompasses the understanding of
the mind, the self, and life. The deeper we
understand, the better control we can have.*

In this chapter, we will dive deeper into how to elicit
desired feelings and moods. Our approach will be similar
to that of positive emotions. However, for every selected
feeling and mood, we will have a short discussion. We
will explore that feeling and mood in some detail. The
following is the summary of the steps.

Step 1: Acknowledge and accept: The first step is to
acknowledge that we need to elicit a positive state of
mind. We need these states in everyday life to achieve the
positive outcomes of our endeavors. Once we accept the
need, the door will open for the analysis, planning, and
execution.

Step 2: Examine and analyze: Ponder about targeted feelings and moods in detail. Let us have a closer look at them. Let us think from a different viewpoint. This is done in this chapter for selected feelings and moods. You may analyze the feelings and moods with reference to intensity and time as discussed in the previous chapters.

Step 3: Plan and act: Once our goal is clear, we may plan as per the classification of intensity and time.

- Low Intensity for Short Time: Use awareness and understanding of situation (use questionnaire given in chapter 16: Questions A to R with appropriate modifications; read and think about the discussion of selected feelings and moods in this chapter).
- High Intensity for Short time: Quick Action tools are useful.
- High Intensity for Long Time: Quick Action and Deep Action tools are needed.
- Low Intensity for Long Time: Deep Action tools are needed.

Note: Please see the "15 steps to implement" given at the end of the chapter on "sadness." Modify them when needed. It might be helpful with appropriate customization for these feelings and moods.

Now, let us explore selected feelings and moods in some detail.

Enthusiasm

If we are alive, why not live enthusiastically?

Once we decide to do something, we may take two approaches out of many approaches. The first one is to feel sorry for one's self, as we need to do this boring thing. The second is to enjoy the activity, as it is the means to a goal which is dear to us. In both the approaches, the common thing is—we need to do the task. The difference is—in the first case, we felt miserable; in the second case, we enjoyed it. So if we have to do something anyway, why not to do it enthusiastically?

Enthusiasm is our intrinsic quality. As a child, we were full of curiosity to know the world. As a child, we were enthusiastic about almost the entire world. Whatever we did, we did with enthusiasm. As we grew, the enthusiasm somehow moved to the back burner. Now is the time to bring back the curiosity and enthusiasm that is our intrinsic nature.

Winston Churchill said, "Success is the ability to go from one failure to another without losing the enthusiasm." We all fail at some point, in one way or the other. Successful individuals are those who maintain the spirit and work with enthusiasm.

We watch many reality shows on television. What differentiates the outstanding anchors from ordinary anchors is the enthusiasm and energy with which they host. Have you listened to teachers, professors, public speakers? What quality stands out in effective speakers?

Of course, the enthusiasm, zeal, passion, and vigor with which they talk. And what kind of people would you like to associate with at your job, in social circles, and in personal lives—people with pessimistic views or people full of energy?

Enthusiasm is the oil which burns the lamp of happiness and progress in our life. It is how life blossoms. It is also contagious. So, let us live with energy, vitality, and vigor and induce the same feeling in the people around us.

Satisfaction

The grass looks greener on the other side of the fence. Many times, we do not appreciate what we have achieved. We do not enjoy the achievements. We rather focus on what we have not achieved or on what other people have achieved, and we become dissatisfied with our lives.

Please note that I am not advocating the feeling of complacency. Let me clarify these two words from my viewpoint. When I say satisfaction, I mean a feeling of happiness about our own accomplishments. Satisfaction means appreciating what we have, enjoying what we have, and celebrating what we have achieved. Satisfaction does not stop us from initiating new endeavors and working hard to achieve them. When I say complacency, I mean I don't what to do any other thing; I become inactive and do not progress any further.

So, how does one elicit the feeling of satisfaction? Observe what you have achieved. Compare it with the achievement of a person with a similar background. If you list ten things, you may find that you have achieved more in at least two to five things. One can't be a winner everywhere and in all the aspects of life. So, if you have achieved more at least in two aspects of life compared to others, you have something to be happy about. And of course, this should not stop you from working hard to achieve more in life.

I asked a student if she was happy with her academic achievements of the last year. She was one of the top five students in her class in a premier school. She replied that she was happy and satisfied with her achievement. To be in the top five students in a premier school is satisfactory performance. She celebrated her achievement. At the same time, she said that she was now full of enthusiasm and aiming to be in the top two this year.

If you had set a realistic goal and achieved it, you should feel satisfied. Next time, you set a higher goal and stretch yourself to achieve even bigger heights.

Perseverance

A farmer bought a new farm which had no well. So, in search of water, he dug ten feet at one place but could not find water. So, he changed the place. At another place, he again dug ten feet. There too, he could not find water. He repeated this process many times. He dug many wells but could not find water. A wise man was passing by his farm. Looking at the farmer's situation, he advised, "Don't dig so many wells. Dig one well deep enough, and you will find the water." If we try one thing for some time and don't get results, we may change to another thing, and keep changing without getting any results. But if we are persistent, determined, resolute, we will eventually succeed in many of life's endeavors.

Once in a while, we may get quick results. Sometimes, we do the right thing at the right time in the right way under the right circumstances and get the right result right away. But this may not happen always. The road to success will test our strength. We may fail initially. Many great achievers have failed in the initial phase of their lives. We might become subject to criticism and even ridicule, but we need to believe in ourselves and be persistent. When I go hiking, I occasionally stop by springs. The gentle flow of water pleases me. I observe that this gentle water flow, persistently flowing over a long period of time, is capable of cutting the hard stones on which they flow. A spring, a gentle flow of water, can also leave behind its mark on the hardest of stones, if it flows persistently.

The quality of perseverance, the feeling and mood to remain consistent over a long period of time, in the midst of difficulties, is what we need to cultivate.

> In the darkest hours of life,
> When all efforts for success have failed,
> When no ray of light seems possible,
> I look at a child,
> The dawn of a human life.
>
> She failed hundreds of times
> While learning to walk,
> Had injured herself and cried,

Had failed, fallen down many times,
But tried again and again.

At last, that day, she walked steadily,
She took baby steps without falling,
A journey of millions of steps to follow,
But it was not the last steps that made her succeed,
But all the tumbling steps that had failed before.

Self-respect and self-esteem

I heard a Zen story. A Zen master was teaching that the world is perfect. A hunchbacked person stood up in the audience and asked, "Master, I am not normal. I am a hunchback. If you are saying that the world is perfect, why am I not perfect?"

The master replied, "You are the most perfect hunchback I have ever seen."

For respecting one's self, one need not be perfect. No one is perfect in all aspects of life, but all of us can be perfect in our own individual way. And if Mother Nature has made us the way we are, we need to appreciate her. Of course, we should always try to improve our selves, but this journey should never make us feel inferior. We need to respect what we are. Our self-esteem should be maintained.

Deeper understanding of life helps establish self-respect and self-esteem. We all are unique. We all have our strengths and weaknesses. The questions we may ask are, "Do I have high standards of integrity? Do I maintain the standard of my character that I have set?" If I am right, I need not worry about other people's opinion of me. Everyone has their own viewpoint. They have their own definition of a respectful individual. It depends on their social and cultural background. I need to make sure that I do not hurt or exploit others. I need to make sure that I think in a mutually beneficial way when it comes to sharing the success. If I am a good person from the humanistic viewpoint, I need not fit into other's standards of perfection.

We all are different. We can't have common criteria to judge everyone. We are what we are. Self-respect and esteem spring from accepting what we are. There is no need for comparison. Of course, the journey of self-development should always go on.

Sense of wonder and curiosity:

Life becomes richer if we have a sense of wonder and curiosity. Look at a child. Notice the innocent smile. For her, the world is exploration. She can look at a butterfly and be amazed. There is no tension, worry, or anxiety. Why? She looks at the world from a fresh pair of eyes. She does not have strong expectations about what should unfold before her eyes. She learns. She develops and acquires skills. This development is based on her curiosity and willingness to explore the world around her.

This curiosity and sense of wonder is one of the qualities of geniuses. Albert Einstein wondered how he would see the world if he was traveling with a wave of light. This imagination gave birth to the formation of the Theory of

Relativity. Many genius individuals have emphasized the need to have curiosity and a sense of wonder like a child.

Our goal may not be to become Newton or Einstein, but the sense of wonder and curiosity will give us an ability to see things differently. It will make us happy and able to enjoy the world like a child. Like a child, we learn to ask questions, without fearing how stupid the question may look like. Like a child, we will see things without social or cultural "programming" and will challenge the paradigms and beliefs that restrict us from achieving our goals. We will be able to think outside the box. There are many questions and problems in life that are unsolved because of the limits of our thinking process. There are many relations strained because we could not perceive others' viewpoints. There are many boring things in life because we can't see the positive side of things. The sense of wonder and curiosity will lead us to unexplored territory from which we will be better equipped to face difficult problems in life and will remain happy and joyful.

Optimism

Is the glass half-filled or half-empty? Whichever way you look at it, it does not change the water level in the glass. It will not change the quality of water. Objective reality remains unchanged, but the answer does reveal the subjective reality. Seeing a glass half-filled will tell you that the person is positive and optimistic. Things in life are not always in black and white; there are many shades of gray. A person who is optimistic will be able to find out the "white" in the shades of the "gray." Winston Churchill said, "A pessimist sees difficulty in every opportunity. An optimist sees opportunity in every difficulty."

In normal situations in life, most of us are optimistic, but when disasters hit, it tests our optimism. After one or two failures, after one or two betrayals in relationships, after a couple of horrible bosses at work, people may gradually shift toward pessimism. Perhaps no one wants to be pessimistic, but the bitter experiences of life make them pessimistic. This is the time to bring out the inner strength of optimism. This is the time when a person should put aside all that had gone wrong and focus on the positive side. We all fail in some way. We all succeed as well in some way. Difficulties are always around in life. If a person is optimistic, the inner lamp of hope will keep burning and he will eventually succeed.

Henry Ford, one of the industrialists of America, said, "Failure is simply an opportunity to begin again, this time more intelligently." This is the spirit of optimism. We may fail. We may fail several times. But we learn from the failure and keep trying again with improved wisdom.

What happens if we do not choose optimism? Well, this life is precious. If we are pessimistic, we may not get the best out of this life. And when the end is near, we may realize that we missed a better way to live this life. So before it is too late, let us see the glass half-filled.

> When an optimist sees bright light coming out,
>> a pessimist sees the dark shadow it creates.
> When an optimist sees the beauty of the full moon,
>> a pessimist sees the dark patches the moon has.

When an optimist enjoys gentle raindrops,
> a pessimist thinks of the mud it may create.
When an optimist enjoys a colorful sunset,
> a pessimist thinks of the dark night ahead.

Optimist says, "Let me be the first to do it";
> Pessimist says, "No one has done it before."
Optimist says, "Let me face it";
> Pessimist says, "Find ways to ignore."
Optimist says, "I will resolve it";
> Pessimist says, "No one has found its cure."
Optimist says, "Let me handle uncertainty";
> Pessimist says, "Stay away if you are not sure."

If you rise, only then will you fall,
> success and failure are two sides of the coin.
If you trust, only then can you be betrayed,
> relations are like a double-edged sword.
Day and night, birth and death,
> are the cycles of nature.
Depends upon you,
> what you are able to capture.

Self-confidence

If we don't believe in ourselves, in whom should we believe?
A journey of a thousand miles toward success begins with
self-confidence. If we don't believe in ourselves, we can't
take the first significant step. We may not succeed always,
but we should be ready to take the calculated risk. We need
to do all the required homework. We need to prepare the
best for the situation. Once we are in the best position

to face the situation, we need to let go of all the fears of failure. We need to let go of the fear of criticism by others. We need to face the situation wholeheartedly and do the best by working hard and vigorously when required. We need to face new challenges. This is the way we may want to live life and believe in ourselves.

One of the ways to develop confidence is by developing the capabilities, skills, attitude, and character required for any endeavor. If you are a singer and you practice singing for hours every day, you will be confident on the stage. If you are a professional player, and if you have undergone proper physical training and practiced the game you play, you will be confident when you go out to play on the field.

You may do mental rehearsals by imagination. You may study what successful people have done in that situation and acquire those skills. If you grow inwardly, your confidence will grow outwardly.

Once we develop the qualities needed for any goal, the confidence will develop gradually. You may initially plan to accomplish a small task successfully. Then, you may extend the task to a bigger goal. As all small successes accumulate, the confidence gradually grows.

Here is one example. If you are preparing for an exam, study a specific topic and test yourself on that topic alone. Once you succeed, study a few more topics and test yourself again. And when you are comfortable, attempt a practice test. The confidence will gradually increase as your success level increases.

Relaxation and Calmness

> "To the mind that is still, the whole universe surrenders."
>
> —Lau Tzu

When Alexander the Great was marching eastward to conquer the world, he heard that there lived a man who was wise. His name was Diogenes. Alexander went to meet him. Diogenes was relaxing and enjoying the sunlight falling on his body.

"What can I do for you?" asked Alexander.

"Just stand a bit aside and don't obstruct the sunlight falling on me," answered Diogenes. This was a courageous answer to the great and powerful Alexander.

"If I have a second chance, I will become Diogenes," said Alexander.

I wonder why the mighty and powerful conqueror would like to become a poor wise man. I wonder which qualities of Diogenes would have influenced Alexander. Let me guess. I may or may not be perfectly correct. I believe one of the qualities that attracted Alexander would be the calmness, serenity, worry-free, and relaxed life of Diogenes.

Yes, relaxation, calmness, and tranquility are the feelings desired by the greatest of men. We all want to be calm. We all want to be relaxed. This is a feeling for which we work hard. We want to live peacefully. And the paradox is that to be happy and relaxed on weekends and vacations, we accept a hectic life. Many times, we run like crazy during weekdays to become relaxed during weekends. The question is, can we become calm in the midst of the chaos? If we can, then we can not only enjoy the weekends, but also the demanding weekdays. It is possible if we develop a proper understanding of life and the ability to become an observer and witness life situations and circumstances when required. If we can live in the "here and now," the chaos will settle down in the mind and a door of calmness will open wherever we are and whenever we want.

PART VI

MANAGING STRESS

CHAPTER 25

Stress Management

"The greatest weapon against stress is our ability to choose one thought over another."
—William James

What is stress? One simplified way of looking at stress is—stress is the body's response to emergency for the purpose of survival. Stress activates certain changes in the body that are favorable for a survival mechanism.

Suppose a robber with a gun pointing at you is running behind you. The body's first task would be survival. To do so, the body will support all activities that can help it escape. Your thought process for finding the way to run will be enhanced. The muscles involved in running will be supplied adequate energy. The blood flow will increase to supply the necessary chemicals. So, blood pressure, heartbeat, and breathing rate will be impacted.

By virtue of stress response, the body saves itself. What happens if the stress response which is useful for survival is triggered by psychological reasons? What happens if such stress comes chronically and our body parameters like blood pressure and heartbeat are affected chronically? This is undesirable. We don't want to generate stress response due to anxiety created for meeting deadlines, the tension of losing a job, going through a difficult divorce, and so on. When our mind interprets any life situation equivalent to crisis for survival, the body's stress mechanism is activated.

Let us understand what can cause stress. I will begin with the following list and you may add many more reasons that cause stress.

- Improper habits of planning, execution, time management, and procrastination
- Disturbed daily routine and improper sleep
- Chronic health problems in self or immediate family
- Going through treatment of any fatal disease like cancer (self or family)
- Death of a loved one
- Stressed relationships and continual disputes with parents, children, siblings, or spouse
- Going through divorce
- Betrayal by a trusted one
- Severe social insult or humiliation
- Financial crisis due to economy or unexpected expense
- Stressed relation at work with colleagues, subordinates, or management
- Demands to meet unrealistic deadlines at work

- No sense of appreciation for our hard work at a job for a long time
- Job loss
- Relocation to a new place and environment
- Joining a new job in a new and different work culture
- Change in lifestyle due to retirement
- Beginning of new and significant relationships like marriage
- Changes in life followed by childbirth
- Chronic anxiety and worries
- Uncured phobias
- Facing failure at any front, like a one-sided love
- Exam preparation
- Preparing for any game or competition
- Going through a bad patch in a career or in any professional endeavor
- Difficulty in accepting reality when we do not like something
- Worries due to uncertainty in future

What are some effects of stress? Let us summarize them.

- Stress aggravates illness. This is not good for health.
- We may become irritated, intolerant, inflexible, which can harm our relationships.
- We are unable to do our best and this hurts our progress at many fronts.
- Stress may lead one to excessive alcoholism or any other addiction.
- We do not live a happy life.

Now, we know that stress can be building up and causing undesired consequences. How to dissipate the stress? If we are feeling frustrated and tensed, what can we do to come back to the normal state? Consider the following activities that may help reduce stress.

- Walk. Walk fast if you want. Walk for half an hour to an hour.
- Jogging and swimming also helps reduce stress.
- Do aerobic exercises.
- Sleep well. Rest well. Take care of your health.
- Talk to a friend or close one. Discuss what is bothering you and frustrating you.
- Talk to your mentors, elders, and explore your situation. They may find some way out.
- If you feel like crying due to overwhelming anxiety, find a quiet place in your home where you are safe and away from others. Then cry. Vent out all frustration.
- Support others. Help others to manage their stress. Many times, when you are helping others and advising them on what they should do, you realize what can work best for you.
- Pursue hobbies.
- Get involved in creative activities.
- Volunteer for a social cause.
- Learn new things. Example—register in any online free course.
- Keep yourself updated about research in the field of stress and stress management.
- Plan for a trip on a weekend. Explore any natural place.

- Plan vacations. Enjoy them. Take a break from normal routines.
- Many times, strained relationships can be rectified by proper communication. Focus on enhancing communication skills.
- Improve will power. If you have a strong will, you can face difficult situations with inner strength.
- Have a positive outlook on life. Be optimistic. Be grateful for what you have in your life.

What else can help us in reducing stress? The following are some other factors that may help you reduce stress.

Time Management

Everyone on this earth has twenty-four-hour days and 365 days a year. However, many of us are high achievers, while others are average or below average achievers. Ability to manage time is one of the key factors for high achievers.

"At this moment, which activity should I do to justify my optimal utilization of time?" This is the question to ask. The activity depends on our short-term and long-term goals. We need to have a clear vision and plan. It is helpful to have activities planned for the year, for the month, for the days and hours, if required. Once we have a clear goal, we need to put aside the procrastination and execute the plan.

Clearly understand the activity you plan so that you assign the right amount of time for the right activity. If the proper amount of time is not allocated to a specific activity due to any reason, the time pressure will mount. While planning, allocate some time for delays that can be caused by external factors.

Some additional things that may help are as follows:

- Set proper priorities of tasks.
- Avoid procrastination.
- Automate as many activities as you can. For example, can you pay the electricity bill directly from your bank account or credit card?
- Delegate/assign the work to others if possible.
- Multitask when and where applicable.
- Set reminders on e-mail or mobile for specific tasks.
- Develop a social support team.
- Reward yourself for accomplishing things on time.
- Team up with others for appropriate tasks; do things together.
- When you plan, have provisions for tasks not completed on time.
- While planning, allocate appropriate time for events not in our control.
- Make a habit to prepare a "time budget" similar to a financial budget. You may plan how much time you want to allocate for education, career, family, vacation, entertainment, health-related activities, etc.
- Clearly define your short-term and long-term goals.

I remember the story of Albert Einstein. In 1905, he published five papers, including papers on the Special

Theory of Relativity. To formulate the theory of relativity is a Herculean task for any individual by any standard. Do you know what else he was doing at that time? Well, he had a "full-time job" as a "patent clerk." He was married and hence he had family responsibilities. But in the middle of all the required activities, he continued working on understanding the nature of space and time. He had all reasons to procrastinate his work on relativity. He did not procrastinate. He managed time and came out a winner.

We are not Einstein, and at the same time, our tasks are not comparable with formulating the theory of relativity. If we really want, we can manage time. If we are really determined, we can take all possible steps that can prevent stress and make ourselves happy. The choice is ours.

Adaptability and adjusting to the changes

Change is the characteristic of nature. Day changes into night. Summer changes into winter. A child grows and changes into a youth and then an elderly person. Let us list some of the changes that happen around us in various aspects of life.

- Personal Life: health and diseases, aging, hormonal changes
- Family/close relationship: marriage, childbirth, divorce, demise of loved one
- Social life: relocation to new town, shifting in new home, joining new club
- Professional life: change of job, change in management or management policies

- Progress of mankind: advances in information technology, electronics, medicines, transportations means, communication devices
- Other changes: change in economic policies, change in government, changes in society

How good we are in adapting to these changes will determine our ability to minimize stress. How does one develop adaptability? How does one cope with change? The following are a few thoughts that may help.

- Be flexible and open to changes.
- Accept the reality created by the changes.
- Understand that you are not the only person facing the changes. So, in case of any change that has an adverse effect on your life, do not succumb to thoughts like "What will others think?"
- Learn new things. Those who learn, adapt faster. For example, before the Internet, a big chunk of communication was done through posts. After the advent of the Internet, people preferred e-mails. Then social media emerged. If we don't learn the tools of modernity, we will be left behind.
- Always have an eye on the big picture of life.
- Get mentally prepared to face sudden changes and unexpected situations. These changes and situations can be an accident, death, diagnosis of a fatal disease, or financial crisis due to any of the previous reasons. Face reality with courage. Say to yourself, "If I am in this situation anyway and anyhow, let me deal with it in the best possible way."

Those who adapt faster face changes with minimal stress. Adaptability is at the base of evolution. Those species who did not adapt to changes perished. Humans adapted to changes. We already have the capability. Let us utilize it to the fullest.

Having a bigger purpose in life along with everyday life activities

Have you observed how difficult it is for a couple to bring up a child? The period of pregnancy is difficult, especially for the female partner. The event of childbirth can be delicate. After the birth, to take care of the child and the mother also involve a lot of effort. And as the child grows, parenthood is also a busy endeavor.

If you look at all the activities, you may realize how difficult they are! I mean all the effort a couple goes through is quite demanding. There are many incidents that may induce stress. Many of the events during the entire process are stressful, but the couple and the family face all the things happily. Why? Behind all the activities and effort, they have a bigger goal. The goal is to have a child. The goal is to extend the family. This bigger goal generates a mindset which is capable of facing all the circumstances that parents go through. This bigger goal gives them the energy, hope, happiness, and inspiration when things are physically and mentally demanding.

What I learned is—having a bigger goal or goals in life can give us the capacity to face difficulties and stress more effectively. The following are some other examples from everyday life, where bigger goals help a person face stress more effectively.

- Consider a player preparing for a big sports event. The player goes through tough physical training. Many times, he is injured, but his goal is big, and he faces difficulties happily. While playing in the event, he might be injured a bit, but his focus remains on winning, and many times, minor injuries are realized after the game is over. The bigger goal of winning gives him strength to face the stressful situation optimistically.

- Consider an entrepreneur or a person working hard to progress in life. He would be working hard day and night. These efforts are otherwise stressful. It does induce stress. But the hard-working entrepreneur or the person determined to enhance his career faces stress happily and manages it effectively.

If you too have a bigger goal in life, then everyday stress will affect you less. The day-to-day stress will become just a stepping stone for a better future. You will face this stress more positively and manage it well.

Spiritual Life and Prayers

Spiritual life gives a bigger purpose of life. It may give you a framework to understand life. In this framework, it might be easier to handle life situations and events that are otherwise difficult to go through. When you are going through a stressful phase of life, your spiritual group may give you a belongingness and support. The spiritual practice may make you strong and wise to face the difficulties with courage. So, depending upon your understanding of life, choose some spiritual activity.

If meditation connects you to the existence through mind, then prayers connect you to existence through heart. Meditation can have a framework to follow. Prayers might be very personal and spontaneous. Prayers are not only complaints and demands, but they are also a way to express gratitude. Prayers might be a way to talk to the existence, God, or your higher self. You may express your emotions, feelings, and stress in prayers and become free from worries. If prayers help you reduce stress, feel free to engage yourself with this activity.

Forgiveness and Letting Go

> "A weak person can never forgive. Forgiveness
> is an attribute of the strong."
> —Mahatma Gandhi

If we keep grudges in our minds, life may become stressful. Many times, we need to let go of things and forgive others. We may realize that we are being treated in a way that we don't deserve. We may feel that we are going through a life situation that we do not deserve. All these things induce stress. Yes, understand that life may not seem fair to us in many circumstances. And it is completely possible that looking backward, we may be able to find a positive side of today's undesired and difficult situation. So, develop the ability to let go of things and forgive others. This will reduce the stress level and will make you engage in meaningful activities.

Utilize Quick Action tools and Deep Action tools.

We have explored the above tools in detail in previous chapters. We have also understood the classification of emotions, feelings, and moods on the time and intensity index. All our learning is applicable for stress management as well. The questionnaire in the chapter on sadness with desired modification can be useful as well.

Let us determine to manage stress effectively. Let us utilize all our learning in this book. Let us put together all the things that we learned and avoid going through stress. I believe, if we plan properly, if we have a clear understanding of life, we may succeed in managing stress effectively.

PART VII

PUTTING THINGS TOGETHER

CHAPTER 26

Living a Happy Life

I heard an anecdote. There was a man who wrote essays on love. He studied many classic books describing love and started giving speeches on love. Gradually, he became famous. He started writing books and became a famous author. People used to come to consult him regarding their love life.

One day, he fell in love with a young woman. The feeling, the experience, and the excitement of love made him aware that love can't be known by reading books alone. He realized that what he knew were mere words. Without experience, those words had no deeper meaning. After he fell in love, he understood that mere philosophy and intellectual exercises do not necessarily replace the experience.

You have read this book. There are many useful techniques. All these techniques are just information unless these techniques are used when needed. Once utilized and implemented, the information turns into experience and knowledge. If a man spends his life spending no money from his treasure, his life is as good as having no money. Similarly, when we spend our life without implementing the knowledge, life is as good as having no knowledge.

The techniques are simple and easy to implement. Identify where and when you want to utilize them. Identify the emotions, feelings, and moods that you want to work on. Plan and execute the plan. Check your progress periodically. Take corrective actions whenever needed. Learn to manage your mind and live a happy life.

I heard a Zen story once. A Samurai met a great monk. He asked the monk, "What are heaven and hell?"

The monk looked into his eyes. After some moments, he started insulting the Samurai. The Samurai never expected such insults. His anger started growing. He asked the monk to stop, but the monk did not.

The monk told him bitter words that the Samurai had never even heard. With red eyes wide open, heart beating fast, blood pressure rising, the Samurai reached out to take his sword ferociously to attack the monk.

"This is hell." said the monk.

For a moment, everything just froze for the Samurai. He realized what the monk was doing. He looked into the eyes of the monk and they were full of tranquility. There was no intention to criticise. Like a true mentor, the monk was just creating a situation so that the Samurai could learn by experience. His heartbeat and blood pressure became normal. Looking into the deep eyes of the monk, all his anger faded away. He calmed down. There were moments of silence. The Samurai gradually became aware of the "here and now." He experienced bliss.

"This is heaven." said the monk.

Our mind is the door to heaven and hell.
Let us open it in the right direction.